Perfect Positive Thinking

Lynn Williams is a consultant who specialises in helping people to think positively and develop motivation, as well as teaching job-search skills.

Other titles in the *Perfect* series

Perfect Answers to Interview Questions – Max Eggert
Perfect Babies' Names – Rosalind Fergusson
Perfect Best Man – George Davidson
Perfect Brain Training – Philip Carter
Perfect Calorie Counting – Kate Santon
Perfect Confidence – Jan Ferguson
Perfect CV – Max Eggert
Perfect Detox – Gill Paul
Perfect Family Quiz – David Pickering
Perfect Interview – Max Eggert
Perfect Letters and Emails for All Occasions – George Davidson
Perfect Memory Training – Fiona McPherson
Perfect Numerical and Logical Test Results – Joanna and Marianna Moutafi
Perfect Numerical Test Results – Joanna Moutafi and Ian Newcombe
Perfect Party Games – Stephen Curtis
Perfect Personality Profiles – Helen Baron
Perfect Persuasion – Richard Storey
Perfect Presentations – Andrew Leigh and Michael Maynard
Perfect Psychometric Test Results – Joanna Moutafi and Ian Newcombe
Perfect Pub Quiz – David Pickering
Perfect Punctuation – Stephen Curtis
Perfect Readings for Weddings – Jonathan Law
Perfect Relaxation – Elaine van der Zeil
Perfect Speeches for All Occasions – Matt Shinn
Perfect Wedding Planning – Cherry Chappell
Perfect Wedding Speeches and Toasts – George Davidson
Perfect Weight Loss – Kate Santon
Perfect Written English – Chris West

Perfect
Positive Thinking

Lynn Williams

BOOKS

Published by Random House Books 2009

10 9 8 7 6 5 4 3 2 1

First published in Great Britain in 2009 by
Random House Books
Random House, 20 Vauxhall Bridge Road,
London SW1V 2SA

www.rbooks.co.uk

Addresses for companies within The Random House Group Limited
can be found at: www.randomhouse.co.uk/offices.htm

The Random House Group Limited Reg. No. 954009

A CIP catalogue record for this book
is available from the British Library

ISBN 9781847945563

The Random House Group Limited supports The Forest Stewardship
Council (FSC), the leading international forest certification organisation. All our
titles that are printed on Greenpeace approved FSC certified paper carry the FSC logo.
Our paper procurement policy can be found at www.rbooks.co.uk/environment

Mixed Sources
Product group from well-managed
forests and other controlled sources
www.fsc.org Cert no. TT-COC-2139
© 1996 Forest Stewardship Council

Typeset in Minion by Palimpsest Book Production Limited,
Grangemouth, Stirlingshire
Printed in the UK by CPI Bookmarque, Croydon CR0 4TD

Contents

Introduction

Some people are naturally positive thinkers. They seem to have discovered the secrets of optimism, independence and flexibility along with enthusiasm and enjoyment.

They always bounce back no matter what's thrown at them, and they nearly always seem able to set productive goals for themselves, face challenges confidently and persevere in difficult circumstances. They are able to grow and develop by working through problems, remaining self-motivated and self-reliant. They work and play creatively and enjoy relationships – co-operating interactively with others and helping and encouraging them.

Most of us know at least one person we would consider to be a positive thinker, someone who is, on the whole, constructive rather than destructive, upbeat rather than gloomy and friendly rather than hostile. We know they will be encouraging rather than obstructive and enthusiastic rather than disheartening. In short, they are positive rather than negative. They can be relied upon to think and act positively even when life is hard for them, and despite hardships and set-backs, they continue to lead satisfying, happy, useful lives.

So is positive thinking inborn, genetic – a naturally sunny attitude to life? Or is it something that we can all learn to develop?

The answer to both questions is, paradoxically, yes.

Most young children appear to be natural positive thinkers. They are often profoundly optimistic, and their belief in themselves and their abilities is unquenchable, even in the face of discouragement. They seem unimpressed by negative feedback and failure, and are less affected by negative beliefs about themselves than adults are.

This robustness may well be inborn – it would certainly be an advantage for young children to be relatively immune to discouragement, with all the trial-and-error learning they have to go through in the course of growing up.

However, by adolescence most of us have succumbed to a degree of negative thinking, and sufficient pessimism to protect ourselves against failure and disappointment.

Positive thinkers, though, are affected less than most. Although they add a hearty dose of realism to the extreme insouciance of childhood, they still retain several valuable childlike qualities; they tend to disregard failure unless, or until, it is recurrent and unavoidable and they ignore comparisons with others preferring to evaluate themselves on their own terms. They place a higher value on effort and commitment than on ability as a measure of self-worth and, most importantly, they pay little attention to negative occurrences – rather than going over them again and again, they let them fade from their memories quickly and naturally.

As a consequence, it is nearly as hard to demotivate positive thinkers as it is young children, with the result that they are happier and often more productive than the general run of adults.

If it's true that we learn how to be negative pessimists (having been positive optimists as children), it's fair to assume that we can un-learn our acquired negativity by copying the attitudes of natural positive thinkers.

What can we learn from positive thinkers?

Positive thinkers give much more of their time and attention to what is positive than to what is negative. However, they don't just look on the bright side; they take positive steps to ensure that there is ample bright side for them to look upon. Positive thinkers don't just think positively, they act positively too. They have a well-defined set of beliefs, attitudes and behaviours that are characteristic of them and contribute significantly to the way they act and the way they respond to life. The key factors that help to support a positive attitude to living are:

- a sense of purpose

- optimism

- energy

- motivation

- realism.

Positive thinking is very different from wishful thinking. While the wishful thinker dreams their life away imagining how things would be if they were different, the positive thinker has the strength and resilience to take active steps towards their dreams. While the wishful thinker denies there is any problem, the positive thinker squarely faces facts and acts decisively to change the situation. Positive thinkers don't become that way by burying their heads in the sand and pretending that everything is sunshine and roses; they use specific life skills to determinedly take charge of their lives.

These skills can be learned, and the first part of this book looks ways of developing the same positive attitudes that positive thinkers possess. By deliberately emulating the outlook, ideas and behaviour that help them to become positive about their lives, by understanding how they respond to events in their careers and relationships, you can achieve the same results that they achieve.

You will discover how understanding your core values can help you become more decisive and strengthen your sense of purpose; find out step by step how to become an optimist and learn to bounce back from set-backs; recognise your motivating factors so that achievement becomes more effortless; and nurture your physical, mental and emotional energy so that you remain fit and active and more than equal to the things life throws at you.

The second part of this book looks at how you can take a positive approach to gremlins – all the negative things that get in the way of you living positively. Although we may sometimes have little choice about the things that happen to us in life, we do have a choice about how we respond to them. Positive thinkers respond more constructively more of the time. It's not that bad things don't happen to them; it's that they cope better and more affirmatively when they do. By practising doing the same things that they do – consciously copying the attitudes, beliefs and actions that help them to remain positive in the face of difficulties – you can achieve the same positive outcomes that they do.

There are a few key things that are at the root of the negative responses we sometimes acquire, fundamental ways of thinking that are less than helpful in many circumstances. In this part of the book you will discover the limitations the comfort trap might be placing on your life and how you can break free of it; how you can beat negativity and build a positive image of yourself; how you can conquer indecision and move forward confidently as well as how demand thinking and comparison-making can be overcome to increase your confidence and well-being.

How to use this book

How you use this book is up to you. Some people like to start at chapter one and go through it page by page; others like to dip in here and there focusing on whatever takes their fancy. You may want to start with the positive life-skills in part one, but it's possible there are things in part two that touch more of a chord that you'd prefer to tackle first. Please, feel free. There's no right or wrong way of doing it.

Some people might find it useful to keep a notebook specifically for the exercises given in the book so that they can look back at them later and see how and where they've changed and developed. Some people might like to work through the exercises in great detail, while others prefer to just skip through the principles for now and maybe come back to them when the need arises. Again, it's entirely up to you how you do it – sometimes just reading something can give you the spark you need in order to change; sometimes you need to do the exercise in full.

Good luck, however you do it. Here's looking forward – optimistically, energetically and realistically – to the start of your positive new life. First of all, let's look at how positive thinkers get to be that way and how you can achieve the same results as they do.

Part one

The positive approach

1   A sense of purpose

Many positive thinkers have an overall aim or direction in life –
a sense of purpose.

Erica, for example, knows where she's going and what she wants
out of life. She currently works in catering, but her long-term plan
is to start her own party-planning business. She loves parties herself
and has a clear idea of what other people will enjoy. She also knows
what sort of people her clients will be.

Although the possibility of starting her own business is still a
few years off – she has young children and wants to concentrate
on them for the moment – her thoughts, ideas and interests are
geared to her future. She takes advantage of every opportunity
that comes her way, from training to chances to network, building
up her skills and contacts. Her children's parties are already a great
success and a valuable showcase for her creativity. They will be
remembered when she starts her business and help her to secure
those important first few clients. Erica feels very positive about
the future.

Edward, on the other hand, has a talent for woodworking and
would have loved to start his own furniture business, but never
really got round to it. He started working in a furniture factory
intending it to be only short-term, but was quickly promoted into
management. He still makes the odd piece in his spare time but
there's less and less opportunity as his career takes him further

away from his first intention. He has also been cajoled into joining several local committees which leave him even less time.

He sometimes wonders if it would still be possible to set up a business but it's more daydreaming than real planning. In other people's eyes Edward is a success, but Edward himself feels he's achieved very little. He is becoming less positive every day.

It's easy to see that Erica has a sense of purpose and that Edward no longer does.

For people who are naturally positive, it's this sense of purpose that gives order and meaning to their lives. They live with intention, moving purposefully towards desired outcomes and objectives rather than drifting aimlessly, carried along by the eddies and currents of circumstance.

People with purpose seem to be able to work more patiently and productively in pursuit of their aims, and will often work co-operatively with others to accomplish mutual goals. They feel in control of their lives. They know what's important to them and set out to accomplish it. Because they have a clear idea of what they are aiming for, they're often willing to take well-calculated risks in order to achieve it. They're also willing to learn new skills, to experiment and they're also able to approach problems and hurdles creatively.

People with a sense of purpose can:

- make long-term plans

- retain a sense of balance

- focus on what's important to them

- get their wants and preferences met

- have an overview of their direction

- know when they've reached their targets

- take their values and priorities into account

- continually develop their skills and talents

- always have somewhere to direct their energies.

People without a sense of purpose may:

- have to make stop-gap provision

- become driven, obsessive or apathetic

- get bogged down in trivia

- find their needs sidelined

- go round in circles and come to dead-ends

- be unsure of what they've achieved

- find others setting the agenda

- get into a rut

- become frustrated.

It's very easy to develop a negative attitude when you continually have to make stop-gap provisions, get bogged down in trivia, feel frustrated and in a rut, and when you suspect that you're going round in circles and reaching dead-ends while others are setting the agenda and sidelining your needs.

On the other hand, retaining a positive outlook is relatively simple when you can focus on what's important to you, direct your energy into developing your skills and talents, know your wants and preferences will be met, and make long-term plans that take your values and priorities into account.

Why is a sense of purpose important?

There is a great deal of confidence and certainty to be gained from knowing what you want to do and why. When you have a strong, clear overview of your direction, you can relate your actions to an end purpose rather than just undertaking a series of meaningless tasks. You are consequently much more likely to stay motivated and on top of things, and retain a sense of movement and momentum rather than becoming frustrated and stagnating.

You're also much more likely to make effective plans and decisions when you are in pursuit of clear aims. With a definite sense of where you want to go, you can be flexible and creative about how you get there. There's usually more than one route to any objective even when there are set-backs, and you often have several options about how to accomplish a specific purpose. Knowing clearly what you are aiming for allows you to recognise and make use of any opportunities that come your way.

A sense of purpose further fosters a positive outlook by encouraging whole-heartedness rather than half-heartedness and inviting you to do things you really *want* to do rather than the things you *should* do, or that other people think you *ought* to do. It helps you to develop your individual identity and self-expression through following your own ideas and encourages a deeper, wider understanding of yourself and your place in the scheme of things.

Unfortunately, we can get so caught up in the minutiae of everyday life that the overall picture gets lost. We reach the end of the day, week, or even a year feeling that although we've been so busy we've hardly paused for breath, we've still not actually achieved anything. So, in practical terms, having a sense of purpose gives an overview of the situation that makes it easier to:

- know where to put time, talents and effort

- make decisions

- set and achieve goals and targets

- plan effective action

- know when to say no

- prioritise conflicting demands

- weigh up the pros and cons of actions and decisions

- recognise and use opportunities

- evaluate consequences and commitments

- be proactive and take the initiative

- take calculated risks – and calculate the risk in the first place

- have control over your life

- plan a timetable, balance activities and arrange your time effectively

- know what you want to achieve, and recognise when you've achieved it.

Developing a sense of purpose

Having a sense of purpose is one of the major keys to developing a positive outlook on life. Developing a sense of purpose or direction means knowing who you are, where you want to go and why you want to go there.

To do this you need to assess your values and ideas, your roles in life, and your purpose in life. You need to be able to set goals, draw up action plans and establish your priorities.

Your values and ideals

Knowing what is important to you is a crucial first step in deciding your direction in life.

Different things are significant to different people. One person may place a very high value on solitude and time alone; another may feel this much less important than time spent with friends. One person may value security highly, while another values freedom even at the expense of safety. Each individual has a different set of values and prioritises them differently.

What is important to you? Values that other people have often found meaningful include: freedom, security, comfort, honesty, adventure, being needed, independence, animal welfare, trust, variety, integrity, creativity, education, intelligence, peace of mind, nature and environment, family, career, friends, simplicity, truthfulness, achievement, spiritual values, political activity.

Think about the values you hold and write them down. When you make your list consider what is important to you and what ideals you hold. You may find it helpful to ask yourself:

- What am I proud of about myself?

- Which values have meaning to me?

- What do I value in others and want to develop in myself?

- Which values do I want to stand for and be associated with in the world?

These are the answers that Pauline, a young primary school teacher, came up with:

- I am proud of my honesty, creativity, intelligence, cheerfulness.

- The values with meaning for me are career, variety, integrity, self-expression.

- The things I value in others and want to develop are patience, tolerance, commitment to friends.

- The values I want to be associated with are education, simplicity, making a difference.

These are where her strongest drives and most compelling motivations are to be found. A life lived with due consideration of values and ideals is bound to be more positive than one that ignores or marginalises them.

Pauline may wonder, for instance, if getting married and having a family 'ought' to be a higher priority than her career or commitment to friends. Or she may wonder if self-expression is an indulgence deserving little time and attention. One glance at her list of values, however, makes it clear that ignoring these things would probably leave her feeling unfulfilled and unhappy in a life that had little meaning for her.

Your roles

Once you've clarified your values, think about the roles you are asked to play in your life. There are four main areas into which most roles fall:

- career and work

- home and family

- social and community

- personal and spiritual.

Some people's roles fall largely into one or maybe two main areas; others are spread evenly across the board. Some people have many roles, while others focus on fewer. Some people like to concentrate their attention on one area, while others prefer a wider balance. Some people play similar roles in different areas (being a carer, for example, both within the family and in a professional capacity); others have widely differing roles.

Some familiar roles include:

- Career and work – teacher, artist, manager, team member, mentor, leader, ideas person, ambassador, sales person, service provider, designer, key-holder.

- Home and family – carer, friend, parent, grandparent, sibling, child, cook, partner, teacher, nurturer, protector, comforter, home-maker, gardener, dog owner, entertainer, house owner.

- Social and community – friend, neighbour, guide leader, sick visitor, charity fund-raiser, community activist, car owner, local resident, environmental worker.

- Personal and spiritual – artist, hiker, adventurer, student, mediator, personal trainer, catalyst, peacemaker, self-nurturer.

Think about your roles, and think about what you actually *do* in each of them. You may, for example, be employed as a secretary or sales manager. Your roles within that job could include mentor, motivator, administrator, team worker, whatever. You may be a parent, but within that role you could choose to be anything from a protector to a nutritionist, to a coach, to a playgroup leader, to a companion. Within the same role, some people see themselves as an enabler, others as a comforter. It depends on individual values and choices.

List your roles, being as detailed or as broad in your definition of them as you wish. Some areas of your life may break down into several highly specific roles. For others, you may decide that several functions can be grouped together into one encompassing role. It is entirely up to you what you consider a separate, clearly defined and easily recognisable role.

When surveying your roles, you may find it helps to consider:

- your responsibilities

- the positions you hold

- the roles you are required to play in each of these positions

- your responsibilities to yourself

- your leisure-time and personal roles.

Your roles, for example, might be:

- Work – salesperson, manager, display/merchandiser, trainer.

- Home – home-maker, cook, friend, partner.

- Community – treasurer of Sales Association, member of Women in Business, local skittles team member.

- Personal – own fitness trainer, own relaxation consultant.

Matching your roles to your values

When you have decided what your roles are, it can sometimes be quite revealing to cross-match them against your values. This is what Joanna, a mother working as a secretary and part-time phone canvasser did:

VALUES

ROLES	HONESTY	CREATIVITY	CARING	TRUST	SOLITUDE	FAMILY	VARIETY
HOUSEWIFE			√			√	
FRIEND	√		√	√			
SUPPORTER			√	√			
MOTHER	√		√	√		√	
SECRETARY							
TELEPHONE CANVASSER							

In this example there is a very poor match between Joanna's roles and her values. Valued things such as creativity, solitude and variety are being neglected, while the roles of secretary and telephone canvasser fulfil none of the values expressed (although they might have been taken on to provide variety and then proved disappointing).

This an extreme example, but we are sometimes called upon to fulfil roles that in no way reflect our values and ideals. When this happens we need to either bring our values into our roles, or adjust our roles to fit our values.

To express her creativity, for instance, Joanna has several options. She could:

- find a more creative job, even if this meant cutting back on other roles

- be more actively creative in her role of housewife and mother

- make time for creative pursuits by dropping the role of secretary or canvasser

- explore the possibility of a more creative role in her current secretarial job (desktop publishing, leaflet design, press-release writing, etc.).

Positive thinkers can be quite determined about matching their roles and values. When a role doesn't express their values they change it, negotiate it, or as a last resort even dump it!

Your purpose in life

Knowing what your values and your roles are, and having considered how the two complement each other, you are now in a good position to think about your purpose in life.

Being able to summarise succinctly who you are and what your purpose is gives you a useful rule of thumb to make choices and gauge decisions by. It helps to prevent drifting and side-tracking without being either rigid or repressive.

Look over your values and roles and see what suggests itself. Your purpose in life is a deeply personal assertion. It clarifies for you (and you alone) what you feel you are *about*. It can be anything from one line to one page long, but it should be personal, positive and an accurate reflection of your values. Aim for something that looks, feels and sounds right to you, then write it down and put it somewhere where you will see it often.

Here are some examples of what other people have written:

To nurture the pathways of self-expression for myself and for others; to be sensitive to and foster creativity in all its forms; to encourage

and make freely available the means of self-expression in others; to believe in the creative potential of all places, at all times, and in all people.
Arts administrator, tutor and mother

To boldly go where no one has gone before – and bring back photographs.
Photographer and explorer

To maintain the highest standards of self-respect, and to actively ensure that every individual within my circle of influence is treated with thoughtfulness, dignity and consideration.
Disability activist and carer

When you know what your life purpose is, you can plan the things you need to do in order to carry it out. You can plan activities and set goals for yourself, knowing that they reflect your values and ideals. This purposefulness is at the root of the confidence and self-assurance natural to positive thinkers.

Setting goals

Goals are the things you want to do, the things you intend to achieve. Once you know what is important to you, you can define your goals much more clearly and accurately.

Look at your values and your purpose in life, and think about what you want to achieve. Imagine how you might achieve your purpose through one or more of your life roles.

John is an education development manager for a voluntary organisation whose life purpose is: 'To make knowledge freely available to all; to encourage, empower and develop those around me; to hold the highest expectations for all people at all times and to do what I can to help them fulfil those expectations.'

He is always looking out for ways to implement his life purpose and, in line with his values of independence and empowerment, he feels that one of the key roles of his job is to mentor junior staff and help them progress. With this in mind, he set one of his goals:

Purpose (part):	. . . to encourage, empower and develop those around me . . .
Values:	independence, empowerment
Role:	mentor
Goal:	increase Alistair's confidence and organisational skills
Idea:	delegate organising seminar to Alistair.

Here's an example from someone else:

Purpose (part):	. . . to build bridges and find out what we have in common . . .
Values:	honesty, openness, commitment
Role:	friend
Goal:	get closer to Paula
Idea:	arrange to meet for coffee and chat.

Once you have an idea of what your goals are, you can begin to define them more clearly so that you can plan your actions.

SMARTS

Make sure your goals are clear, well thought out and well defined. They need to be:

- **Specific**. Keep goals simple and direct. If a goal seems complicated, break it down into two or three simpler ones.

- **Measurable**. Make sure you'll know when you've achieved your goal. Give precise details so that you know what you are aiming for and include some way of assessing your progress along the way.

- **Attractive**. How do you feel when you think about achieving your goal? Positive? Excited? Is there anything you could add that would make it even more attractive?

- **Responsible**. Make sure your goal is a result of your own actions, not just a hope that things will happen or that other people will do something.

- **Timetabled**. Set a date or have a definite time-frame for your goal. 'Sometime in the future' is an awfully long time away. It will also give you a timetable when you come to plan your actions.

- **Supported**. What support would you like? What resources do you need? Are there people who could help in any way?

John clarified his goal about increasing Alistair's confidence by applying SMARTS. This is what he came up with:

Goal	**To increase Alistair's confidence and organisational skills.**
Specific	Delegate organising the fund-raising seminar in June to Alistair, including participant list mailing and response, finalising the speaker list, drawing up a programme and arranging the venue and catering.
Measurable	Set criteria with Alistair about what 'a successful seminar' means – from his point of view and that of the participants.
Attractive	Very. Mentoring Alistair successfully through this seminar should increase his skills appreciably and it also means I can confidently delegate to him in future.
Responsible	Need to make sure Alistair knows what he has to do and has all the information and resources to do it.
Timetabled	Decide dates with Alistair when each task to be done by; check budget progress; arrange fortnightly meetings between now and June to assess progress.
Supported	Make sure seminar file and contact book available; ditto address list. Contact Jan Gordon and let Sue know so she can help if necessary.

Planning your actions

Next consider the practical steps needed to achieve your purpose. For each of your goals, think about the actions you will have to take to accomplish it. If your goal seems complicated or a long way off, break it down into smaller steps, or targets to make planning easier.

Long-term planning

Long-term planning is no different from short-term planning, it just requires more steps. Be bold and positive when choosing your long-term goals – decide on your goal *then* think about how to get there. Don't let current circumstances limit your dreams.

There are two keys to successful long-term planning. First, when you have long-term goals, plan a series of targets between where you are now and where you want to be. This gives you a series of short steps, rather than one big intimidating jump, between you and your goal. Second, instead of working forward from your current position, work back from your ultimate goal to where you are now.

Sara was enthusiastic about running in a charity marathon even though it was something she had never done before. She wasn't particularly athletic so the task seemed daunting and she wondered if it was actually possible. Sara had a year to prepare, however, and she worked out what she needed to do in the following way. First of all she sketched out her situation:

> Start (I am here): totally unfit.
>
> End goal (I want to get here): run a marathon.

Then she asked herself where she would need to be, and what she would need to be *already* doing, to make her ultimate goal likely. She decided to make this a target:

> Start: totally unfit.
>
> Target: able to run 10 miles relatively comfortably.
>
> End goal: run a marathon.

Now, what would Sara need to be doing already to make this target of running 10 miles achievable?

> Start: totally unfit.
>
> Target 1: jogging 5 miles three times a week.
>
> Target 2: able to run 10 miles relatively comfortably.
>
> End goal: run a marathon.

Sara kept asking the question until she arrived back at where she was now.

The secret is to keep breaking your targets down into smaller and smaller stages until you arrive at steps that you firmly believe you can achieve:

> Values: health and strength; supporting local causes.
>
> Goal: run a marathon to raise money for the local hospice.
>
> Target 1:   jogging 5 miles three times a week.
>
> Mini-targets: 1. walk 20 minutes three times a week by end of June

2. mixed walking and jogging 20 minutes by mid-August

3. jogging 20 minutes by end of September

4. increase distance by x amount each week until Target 1 is achieved.

Actions: get proper footwear

check targets and timetable with fitness centre

plan route

health check with GP

find suitable warm-up exercises.

Prioritising

Knowing what to do is essential. Knowing what *not* to do is quite useful too.

When you are clear what your life purpose is, prioritising demands and tasks becomes much more simple. You need to ask yourself, does this contribute to my purpose in life? If yes, then do it; if no, then don't do it.

If you're still undecided, or you're not sure if what's come up is a genuine opportunity or just a side-track, consider your values and roles. Think of your roles and values as a grid:

	ONE OF MY VALUES	NOT ONE OF MY VALUES
ONE OF MY ROLES	area 1	area 3
NOT ONE OF MY ROLES	area 2	area 4

Area 1 is the most important. Anything that reflects both your values and your role in life is clearly a high priority and should get the lion's share of your time and attention.

Area 2 is the next most important. Something that relates to your values, even if it isn't currently one of your roles, should be thought about. Even if you can't take on the appropriate task yourself, could you delegate to somebody who can?

Area 3 is less important. It may be a task that falls within your role, but if it's not in line with your values, dispatch it efficiently, then look at how it's arisen and see if there's something you can do to stop it coming up again.

Area 4 tasks and demands are your lowest priority, reflecting neither your values nor any of your roles. Keep them to a minimum and dispatch them speedily. If tasks in this quadrant keep growing, you may need to plan a major lifestyle shake-up.

Putting it all together

Take some time to think about and plan your direction. It's worth actually writing down your aims and objectives to clarify your mind, and also to put them 'out there' rather than just keeping them in your own head. Keep a notebook or loose-leaf folder and use a fresh page for each of the following headings:

- My values

- My purpose in life

- My goals for the next 5 years

- My goals for this year

- My goals for the coming 3 months

- My main priority this week

- Today's priorities.

Review and update your objectives regularly, and remember to congratulate yourself when you stick to a priority and/or achieve a goal.

Recap

Positive thinkers have a sense of purpose. Enhance your natural sense of purpose.

- Decide on your purpose in life:

  - Understand what your values are.

  - Understand what role you play.

  - Make sure your roles reflect your values.

  - Make a personal, positive declaration stating your life's purpose.

- Set goals to achieve your purpose in life.

- Plan actions to achieve your goals.

- Prioritise your activities.

2 Optimism

Optimism is the ability to see the positive side of things rather than the negative. Optimistic thinkers are usually positive people because they approach life with the expectation that a happy outcome is both desirable and possible. Optimists are sometimes mistakenly accused of wearing rose-tinted spectacles – of believing that everything will turn out for the best in the end, so why worry? True optimism, however, doesn't just mean turning a blind eye to problems, it means actively searching out the positive factors in the situation.

Steven was made redundant when the company he worked for was taken over. As he was in his fifties, everyone told him he was unlikely to find another position. Taking stock of his situation, Steven decided he had nothing to lose by continuing to apply for the sort of job he was used to doing, but that he would look into other possibilities as well. His great love was photography and, although work commitments left him little time to pursue it, he thought that this might be his opportunity to focus on his hobby and turn it into something more.

He'd sold several pictures of local events to newspapers and agencies in the past and decided he could build on this success. After several months' hard work, he'd made more sales and built up a useful list of contacts. A course in portrait photography gave him more ideas and opened up further possibilities. Although his job applications never found him a job like his old one, they did result in an interesting part-time position he would never have considered before but which now suited him better. Eighteen months on from redundancy, Steven considers the whole thing to have been a blessing in disguise and feels very positive about his future.

Optimists anticipate success and look for evidence of it. Pessimists, on the other hand, anticipate failure and look for evidence of *that*. Consequently, when things go wrong – and even optimists will admit that things go wrong occasionally – pessimists will say, 'There you are, what did I say? I'm a real failure.' Optimists, on the other hand, will indignantly look for the reasons *why* it went wrong, and do things differently in the future as a result.

Optimists are often:

- confident, adventurous and willing to take chances

- open, outgoing, approving of others and broadminded

- energetic, productive and positive

- enthusiastic, vibrant, light-hearted and relaxed

- in control and buoyant.

Pessimists tend to be:

- anxious, apprehensive and timid

- defensive, critical, suspicious and withdrawn

- passive, dependent and negative

- alarmist, gloomy, despondent and tense

- fatalistic and fearful.

Why is optimism useful?

Seeing the positive aspects of difficult or disappointing circumstances gives optimists the courage and ability to carry on and try again. They can learn from mistakes and apply that knowledge to subsequent events, rather than either avoiding similar situations in future, or fatalistically repeating the same errors.

Optimists look at their lives in terms of success rather than setbacks. They focus on what they have achieved, however little, rather than dwelling on what might have been and where they have failed. They also have a much broader definition of success than pessimists, taking any sign of progress as evidence of achievement.

This means that optimists are able to maintain a healthy self-esteem – they 'fail' less often. They can be more flexible and creative in the face of set-backs and deal with problems rather than avoiding them. They tend to explore opportunities more thoroughly and extensively, taking greater and better-calculated risks. They maintain higher expectations of themselves and others, retain their energy and motivation and enjoy their own and others' achievements.

Developing optimism

Some people may be born optimists, but for those of us who aren't, it is still possible to achieve a much more optimistic outlook on life.

Psychologists looking into optimism found out that optimists shared many of the same attitudes to success and failure, and that these were very different from the attitudes of pessimists. In particular they found that optimists believe that:

Success is:

- Permanent – once a success, always a success.

- Individual and inner-directed – success is a result of personal character and effort.

- Generalised – success in one thing means success is possible in all things.

Whereas failure is:

- Temporary – it's just this time and won't last.

- Due to outside factors independent of the individual.

- Specific – just because one thing fails it doesn't mean that others will.

Interestingly, they found that pessimists believe exactly the opposite. They assume that failure is:

- Permanent – once a failure, always a failure.

- Individual and inner-directed – failure is a result of personal characteristics.

- Generalised – failure in one thing means failure is inevitable in all things.

And that success is:

- Temporary – it's just this time and won't last.

- Due to outside factors independent of the individual.

• Specific – just because one thing succeeds it doesn't mean that anything else will.

You can increase your positive thinking by deliberately adopting the optimists' way of looking at things. Doing this consciously and persistently, you can gradually change your habits of thinking and achieve a more optimistic and positive frame of mind.

Focus on your successes

You need to focus on your successes and acknowledge and enjoy them, and minimise your failures, putting them into perspective. Consciously search out and notice success and pleasure in your life. Change any negative thoughts that accompany success or enjoyment into positive ones. Remember what optimists firmly believe:

Success is permanent. Replace any ideas that success won't last with a positive appreciation of its permanency:

NEGATIVE THOUGHT	POSITIVE THOUGHT
I was lucky that time.	I usually succeed.
It was just a fluke, it won't last.	I've done it once; I can do it again.
I'm having a good time for once.	I usually enjoy myself.
I made a good impression, but it won't last.	I've made a good beginning, I can build on it.

Success is individual and inner-directed. Substitute any negative thoughts about it being just a lucky chance with ones that acknowledge your skill and effort:

NEGATIVE THOUGHT	POSITIVE THOUGHT
It was just luck.	I planned well and was prepared.
It was lucky that time.	I worked hard for it and I deserve it.
It was a lucky chance.	I saw the opportunity and seized it.
It was the rest of the team that won.	I played an important part in our success.

Success is general. When you succeed in one thing, remind yourself that you will succeed in other things too:

NEGATIVE THOUGHT	POSITIVE THOUGHT
James likes me.	I'm a likeable person.
That was easy.	I'm good at this.
That meeting was OK.	I'm effective in meetings.
I managed to do that bit.	I'll be able to do the rest of it now.

Minimise your failures

Consciously put your failures and disappointments into perspective against a positive background. Remember what optimists always remind themselves:

Failure is temporary. Replace catastrophic 'always and never' thoughts with more positive ones:

NEGATIVE THOUGHT	POSITIVE THOUGHT
I'm stupid. I don't understand this.	I don't have enough information.
I'm slow and incompetent.	I don't have the right equipment.
I'm no good at making decisions.	I don't have the right advice yet.
Everything's my fault.	There are a number of reasons why we failed.

Failure is specific. Substitute positive thoughts for any generalised 'nobody, nothing, never' ones you may have:

NEGATIVE THOUGHT	POSITIVE THOUGHT
Nobody likes me.	It's not easy getting to know people here.
I'm stupid.	I'm not familiar with this particular subject.
Nothing ever works.	This particular thing didn't work.
Life is hard.	This specific problem is a challenge.

Look for positive features

When you're confronted with a negative solution – a disagreement, for example, a disappointing result, or something that hasn't quite worked out – actively and consciously look for the positive elements before wading into the negative criticism.

Adopt the 'PIN' code and evaluate the situation in the following order:

P   First look for something **positive** about it.

I   Next look for something **interesting** about it.

N   Only when you've done that, look for anything **negative** about it.

Penny had been on a diet that hadn't worked out. She decided to apply the PIN code to assess what had happened:

Positive	I had the will-power to keep to it for one week.
	I lost 1 pound.
	I started to feel more energetic.
Interesting	I discovered some new low-fat recipes.
	I learned more about a healthy diet.
	I found out where the local swimming pool was.
Negative	I went back to my old habits after a week.

When Tina was faced with an unavoidable move to a new area when her partner was promoted, she used the PIN code too:

Positive	Opportunity to explore new places.
	Chance to make new friends.
	Opportunity to leave old habits behind.

Interesting	Chance to see how I cope with change.
	Chance to think about what I want for the future.
Negative	Saying goodbye to old friends.
	Leaving the safe and familiar.

Focus on solutions

When you know what the negative aspects are – having already found out the positive and the interesting ones – don't just dwell on them, work out what went wrong and decide how you will do things differently in the future. Look for solutions.

For example, Penny realised that the negative solution was that she went back to her old eating habits after a week, so she came up with the following solutions to make sure her diet was more successful in future:

- recognise 'danger zones' and plan accordingly

- team up with a friend for support

- plan plenty of activities

- plan and buy two weeks' food at start

- remember never to shop when hungry

- plan fitness-related activity to boost metabolism in second week.

Tina also had some ideas about dealing with the negative aspects of moving to a new area:

- find out about the new place before moving

- visit for the day

- write to local branch of professional society

- remember that everywhere becomes familiar after a while.

Adopt broadminded attitudes

There are usually several ways to interpret situations, particularly when it comes to other people's behaviour. Optimists generally adopt the most broadminded and favourable ones, and give people the benefit of the doubt wherever possible. Before automatically deciding what something 'means', think consciously about the other possible interpretations.

For example, if a friend is irritable and brusque, a negative interpretation might be 'She doesn't like me anymore', but a more positive explanation might be that she's worried about something. When a partner is feeling tired and run down, a negative worry might be that he's sickening for something, but it might be simply that he's been very busy recently. And an employer who is unusually critical might be looking for a reason to sack you, but it may just be that they're under pressure too.

Act on the most generous interpretation

Unless, or until, they have evidence to the contrary, optimists act as if their most benign interpretation of the situation was the true one. Follow their lead and consider how you can act positively. Here are some examples, using the situation outlined above:

- A friend is irritable and brusque. The positive interpretation is that she's worried about something, so decide to stay friendly towards her and make sure there's an opportunity to talk if she wants to.

- Your partner is feeling tired and run down. The positive interpretation is that he's been very busy recently, so take the weekend off to relax and decide to take responsibility for some of his chores.

- An employer is unusually critical. The positive interpretation is that they're under pressure too, so be extra diligent and pleasant at work to take off some of the stress.

Recap

Positive thinkers have optimism. Enhance your natural optimism.

- Focus on pleasure and success:
  - success is permanent
  - success is due to your own individual talent and hard work
  - success is general.

- Minimise your failures:
  - failure is temporary
  - failure is due to outside factors
  - failure is specific.

- Look for all the positive things first.

- Focus on solutions.

- Adopt broadminded attitudes.

- Act on the most generous interpretations of events.

3 Energy

Energy is that liveliness and vigour with which some people approach their activities. It's both the physical expression and a fundamental component of the enthusiasm they seem to infuse into everyday life.

Energy has two major aspects: zest and stamina. Zest is the get-up-and-go that initiates activity and stamina is the resilience that allows activity to continue. Energy that has both these components confers a high degree of indefatigability and buoyancy on the lucky recipient, making them not only lively and active with a relish for life, but resistant to stress and illness and able to bounce back from knocks and set-backs.

Why is energy useful?

People who are positive frequently have a high degree of physical robustness and resilience. To some extent this may be the result of their positive attitude, rather than the cause of it. However, there's no denying that you need energy and resilience to do the things you want to do and to maintain a positive outlook on life. Constant tiredness and aches and pains, or feelings of being 'out of sorts' and 'below par' limit your activities and significantly reduce your quality of life.

A sense of purpose and an optimistic outlook are, in themselves, great energisers. But energy needs a firm physical platform as well. The physical capacity, as well as the mental and emotional ability, to get through the day with direction, determination and spirit depends on fostering the optimum conditions for health and fitness, and treating your body with tolerance and respect.

Although we may not be able to completely avoid illness, accidents and old age – human life unfortunately just isn't like that – we can take care of our physical health in such a way as to achieve the maximum sense of well-being whatever our circumstances.

Developing energy

There are few magic potions or miracle cures. Developing energy and vitality depends on the ordinary, everyday principles of good nutrition, adequate exercise and sufficient rest. Adopting simple good habits in these areas can, however, bring about a seemingly miraculous improvement, especially if your body has been used to running on empty.

Instant lifts

Beware of some things that seem to promise an instant energy boost. Tea and coffee, for example. A strong cup of coffee or tea is still one of the most popular pick-me-ups. One cup is fine, but beware of using it to compensate for more serious energy depletion. Sugar is also one to be wary of. A sugary snack can, paradoxically, lower blood-sugar levels, which will leave you feeling tired and depressed after a brief buzz. And definitely beware of alcohol, which will do little to actually raise your energy and will cause a deterioration in performance.

If you need a quick burst of refreshment try these instead:

- Fresh air. A few deep breaths of fresh air outside or at an open window will wake you up and keep you going.

- Starch. Better than sugar for providing energy, starchy foods release their sugars over a longer period without swamping your system. Wholemeal bread, cereals, bananas and dried fruit are all good energy providers.

- Music. Put on some fast, upbeat music for extra pep. If you find yourself singing or tapping your feet, even better.

Stress

The biggest threat to energy is stress. A little of it can add a bit of spice to life; too much is a major problem. Luckily there are several methods of keeping stress under control.

First of all, look after yourself. Don't put extra stress on your body by asking it to cope with a poor diet, too much alcohol, or too many cigarettes. Exercise regularly, as it not only helps release frustration and tension in the short term, it also helps to strengthen the body against the long-term effects of stress.

Take breaks. It sounds obvious, but don't forget to take breaks at regular intervals. Things can seem so urgent and important that holidays, rest and enjoyment drop right to the bottom of the list as 'non-essentials'. You'll find you have more time to take breaks if you're assertive about what you are and are not going to do. Don't say 'yes' or 'maybe' when you mean 'no'. Don't put up with people treating you badly; tell them politely but firmly to stop. After all, nothing is worth putting up with if it makes you ill.

When faced with a problem, take a deep breath. When stressed, breathing tends to be rapid, shallow and high up in the chest. To relax, breathe slowly and deeply, using all of your chest right down to your stomach. Then try to get to the root of the issue. Find out what's causing the stress and plan positive action to overcome it with someone you trust. Just putting it into words often helps to put things into perspective and makes them easier to deal with.

In general, make time to relax. Just 5 minutes, morning and evening, spent consciously calming down and letting go of tension can make an enormous difference. And try to laugh more. Strange but true: even a false smile and false laughter have a relaxing and enlivening effect on the body.

Accept that stress is part of life – however nice it would be, the time will probably never come when life is completely free from stress or worry. Knowing that you can meet the challenge and deal with stress is more positive than living in fear of it.

Optimum energy

To increase your energy levels, make the most of your physical health, and maintain and increase well-being: eat a balanced diet, exercise regularly and remember the three 'R's: rest, relaxation, recreation. These factors are to some extent interdependent. You will, for example, sleep better when you take regular exercise. If, however, you have any doubts about your health, or are uncertain about the wisdom of changing your diet or starting to exercise, then see your GP who will be able to advise you accordingly.

Eat a balanced diet

Just a few very simple changes can turn the average diet into a healthy eating plan. Eat more fibre – choose complex carbohydrates such as wholemeal bread, pasta, oats, brown rice, beans and the humble potato. Get more vitamins, ideally from fresh fruit and vegetables rather than supplements (five portions a day is the recommended amount). And increase the amount of low-fat protein in your diet – opt for chicken and fish more often, grilled or baked, not fried.

Decrease the amount of fat you consume – make use of the low-fat alternatives to butter and margarine. Replace milk, yogurt and cheese with low-fat semi-skimmed varieties. Cut back on fried food and save cream, crisps and chocolate for special occasions. Gradually reduce the amount of sugar you add to tea and coffee – and try to drink fewer caffeinated drinks in any case, replacing them with fruit juice or water when possible. Watch out for added sugar in prepared foods.

In addition, eat a good breakfast – cereal, fruit or wholemeal toast will give you an energy boost at the start of the day. Take time to eat properly, trying not to skip meals or eat on the run. It's important to give yourself a break and enough time to digest your food properly. Eat a varied diet, not relying on the same menu day after day. The wider the range of foods you eat, the better. And avoid sugary, fatty snacks. Whether you eat the traditional three square meals or four or five smaller ones, eat well at your regular meal times so that you don't feel hungry in between.

Exercise regularly

Adopting the habit of taking a little regular exercise will pay big dividends in terms of fitness. It's surprising just how little is required for basic health. It's helpful to think in terms of three main areas: your vital organs (i.e. heart and lungs), suppleness and muscle strength.

For your heart and lungs, you need some aerobic activity that makes you slightly out of breath. Twenty minutes to half an hour of brisk walking, cycling or swimming three times a week will do. Every day would be even better, and would help to build up your stamina. Gentle stretching will help to keep your body free from stiffness, aches and pains. Ten minutes three times a week will keep you supple, or every morning if you prefer. And include some form of exercise that requires you to use your strength once or twice a week. This could include natural activities such as digging the garden or chopping wood.

As well as taking time for specific exercise, you can also improve your general fitness by being a little more active in your day-to-day activities. Use the stairs instead of waiting for the lift, walk to the shop instead of taking the car, bicycle to work or unwind occasionally by going for a walk instead of sitting watching television.

You can enjoy yourself as well. Dancing, energetic play with children, sport and kick-about games are all excellent ways of maintaining fitness. It is regular, habitual gentle exercise that reliably builds stamina, suppleness and strength, however, rather than the occasional weekend splurge.

Rest

There are three main things that contribute to balanced rest and relaxation. Sleeping well, waking up refreshed, and staying relaxed during the day.

Different people need different amounts of sleep. Some are happy and refreshed after just 5 or 6 hours, others feel deprived if they don't get 8 or 9. The amount of sleep is less important than its quality. Recharge your batteries and get good quality sleep.

Aim to get to bed at the same time every night – your body clock can be thrown by random bedtimes and make it harder for you to get to sleep. Establish a routine for winding down before bed, which could include reading a book, listening to restful music and taking a bath. Your mind and your body will both appreciate clear signals that the time for sleep is approaching. Avoid caffeine in coffee and tea before bed, and be very cautious with alcohol. Hot milk or herbal teas are preferable, but if you tend to wake in the night to go to the lavatory, avoid late-night drinks altogether. Avoid eating a heavy meal shortly before going to bed, but don't go to bed hungry either.

Make sure the room where you sleep is well ventilated, not too hot and reasonably dark. If noise is a problem, earplugs are a comfortable, effective and economical solution. Ensure the bed is comfortable and your bedding warm. Keep the room just as a bedroom, if at all possible. You need to associate going to bed with going to sleep, so bedrooms that are also used as offices or recreational rooms can sometimes cause problems. Unless your GP advises otherwise, avoid sleeping pills. Reserve them for short-term use in exceptional circumstances.

If you have trouble getting to sleep, or wake soon after dropping off, wait a quarter of an hour, then get up and do some undemanding activity for a bit (doing the ironing seems to be very popular). If worries or a racing mind are keeping you awake, write down your thoughts on a piece of paper then put it aside with the promise you'll deal with it in the morning. After a short while, go through your usual winding-down routine and prepare to go to sleep again. Make sure that you are physically comfortable and that hunger, heat or cold aren't keeping you awake. Whether you sleep or whether you don't, get up at your usual time the next day rather than sleeping on. If sleeplessness is a persistent problem, speak to your GP about it.

Get a good start to your day. Wake up feeling refreshed, relaxed and alert: Try to wake up at the same time every day, even on weekends and holidays. Avoid over-sleeping; it can make you feel heavy and headachy and upset your natural sleep patterns. If you need extra sleep, go to bed earlier rather than sleeping late. Remember to let your body know it's daytime: give it light, air and movement. Open the curtains or turn on lights in winter. Don't try to get dressed and ready in dim lighting, your body will be uncertain whether it's day or still night. Get some fresh air. Open the window and take a few moderately deep, slow breaths. (If it's below freezing exercise caution; a sudden shock of cold air can be harmful to some conditions.) Move your body. Gentle, undemanding stretching exercises will release tension and get your blood circulating. If you can, fulfil all these requirements by getting out into the fresh air and natural light for a short walk before breakfast.

Relaxation

Being tense uses up valuable energy. By staying calm and relaxed, you can use that energy more effectively.

Develop the habit of staying relaxed throughout the day. Check for tensed muscles every so often. Look for tense stomach muscles, hunched shoulders, a habitual frown, etc. Consciously let those muscles relax. Check your breathing. Relax your chest by taking a deep breath in and letting it out slowly. If you're in a situation where you feel yourself becoming stressed, angry or upset, breathe in, counting slowly to three, and breathe out again before saying or doing anything. If you're becoming flustered, deliberately slow down. Be aware of the things that put extra stress on your body, such as caffeine in tea, coffee and cola drinks, sweets and sugar and junk food in general, as well as alcohol.

As well as checking for tension, take time each day to practise consciously relaxing, both physically and mentally. Each of the following exercises takes around 5 to 10 minutes to complete. If you have more time though, take as long as you like. Relaxing music or a tape of natural sounds can also help set the mood.

Physical relaxation

One of the easiest ways to release physical tension is to deliberately tense and relax each group of muscles in turn:

Sit or lie in a quiet, comfortable place where you won't be disturbed. Begin by taking a deep breath in and letting it out slowly. Just enjoy letting go and breathing quietly for a moment. Beginning with your feet, tense the muscles for a second or two and then let go and release the tension. Tense the muscles in your legs and then let go. Continue all the way up your body, tensing and relaxing your muscles. Finally squeeze your face muscles into a tight grimace and then let go and relax. Remain quietly relaxed for a few moments, breathing slowly and gently.

Mental relaxation

You can either continue on from the previous exercise while lying quietly relaxed, or do this separately:

Make yourself comfortable. Close your eyes and think of somewhere ideal for relaxing – the beach, perhaps, or a garden. Imagine you are actually there. Enjoy the sights and sounds and scents around you. Feel the warm sun on your skin; hear the gentle waves or the soft rustle of leaves. If any thoughts intrude, simply notice them and then let them go. Bring your thoughts back to the peaceful place you are imagining. Imagine your body being refreshed as you enjoy the peace and calm. After 5 or 10 minutes, open your eyes. Take a deep breath and let it out slowly. Have a good stretch. Sit up or get up in your own time.

Recreation

Recreation is a very simple and often-neglected part of a healthy life. In order to recharge your batteries, you need to set aside time to be alone with yourself, do things that give you pleasure and spend time with people who like you.

Be alone with yourself

Take time to get to know yourself. Find out what your own moods and rhythms are when you're away from the influence of other people. You could:

- take yourself for a walk
- take yourself away for the day to explore a new place
- curl up with a good book
- paint a picture
- write in your diary
- listen to music
- go through your photograph album.

Be kind to yourself, nurture yourself, and plan treats for yourself, just as you would for any other best friend.

Do things that give you pleasure

Doing things you enjoy sounds very obvious, but it's just the sort of thing that gets pushed to the bottom of the list when you're busy or stressed.

Make a list of all the things that give you pleasure, and

consciously remind yourself to do them regularly. Include a range of things that are:

Exciting

- adventure – travelling, exploring, trying new things
- sports – team games or individual physical activity to enjoy a sense of exhilaration and movement
- challenges – physical challenges, running, hiking, climbing, orienteering, sailing.

Creative

- exercising your talents – musical, artistic, dramatic, practical, intellectual
- going to the theatre, art galleries, cinema
- painting, sculpture, photography
- writing poetry, fiction, letters, articles
- playing music, listening to music
- developing crafts.

Stimulating

- learning new things – skills, languages, new topics, hobbies and interests
- computer games
- word games and puzzles
- quizzes and competitions.

Rewarding

- volunteer work
- charity work
- community projects.

Practical

- gardening
- cooking
- DIY and decorating.

Sociable

- family visits and get-togethers
- time with friends
- children's activities
- groups and societies.

Relaxing

- meditating
- enjoying nature, walking, bird-watching
- unwinding, sitting by the fire, lying in a hammock.

Spend time with people who like you

Make sure you see people whose company you enjoy. This is another of those things that can get overlooked in a busy schedule, but time spent with friends is essential to well-being.

Nurture friends carefully and make most of your relationships. Take a genuine interest in your friends, ask them questions and listen to their answers. Share their enthusiasm and be glad when they're happy. Let down your barriers and be open with them and be ready to offer and receive support. Be generous with both apologies and forgiveness when needs be and be willing to be forgiven too. Be what you would like others to be – loyal, sensitive, discreet, whatever. Display in your own behaviour the qualities that you value in others. Above all, let your friends know that you like them.

Recap

Positive thinkers have energy. Enhance your natural energy:

- Be wary of instant lifts.

- Keep stress under control.

- Eat a balanced diet – increase your intake of fruit, vegetables and complex carbohydrates and decrease your fat intake.

- Take regular exercise – 20 or 30 minutes, three times a week, minimum.

- Get enough rest.

- Relax.

- Make time for recreation.

4 Motivation

Motivation is the urge to achieve aims and reach goals. It's the persistent drive that gets you through the difficult patches and impels you to attain your objectives. It's the ability to maintain an interest, and a sense of direction and forward movement towards a desired outcome. It's the underlying, inherent reason why you do anything at all, ever.

Claire and Nicholas were both taking an evening course studying French at their local college. Claire often holidayed in France and enjoyed its culture and people so much she was seriously thinking about living there. Although she had done quite badly in languages at school, she had picked up a few words from her travels and was sure she was capable of learning more. Although she found the work challenging, she was determined to surprise and delight friends she had made in France by speaking to them in their own tongue.

Nicholas, on the other hand, was studying because he thought it might come in useful in the future even though he had no definite plans to visit France. He was actually beginning to find the course work rather a chore and wondered whether German wouldn't have been a better choice as the company he worked for had several German clients. He made a few enquiries about changing courses but never went back after the Christmas holidays. Afterwards, he felt it was just one more thing that he'd failed at.

The main difference between Claire and Nicholas was that Claire was highly motivated while Nicholas wasn't.

Different people have different motivations, and what motivates one person can often leave another cold. Your individual motivation will depend largely on your personal values, but some of the key factors inherent in the desire to get something done are:

- Emotional attraction – you will rarely persevere with something you don't feel strongly about.

- Courage – a degree of personal courage and perseverance are needed to take the initiative and start projects, and to overcome obstacles and set-backs along the way.

- Optimism – the positive expectation of a successful outcome is needed in order to start in the first place.

- Energy – feelings of low physical energy and impaired resilience quickly sap the will to take action.

- Purpose – vision and a sense of mission give purpose and direction, and help to maintain motivation over the long term.

Why is motivation important?

Motivation is what takes dreams and plans and turns them into reality. Positive thinkers are very good at getting motivated and staying motivated. They have mastered the art of self-motivation, and use that skill to put their best effort into whatever they do.

This makes them enviably independent. They are clear about what they want to do and why they want to do it. Because they have a clear idea of how what they want fits in with their values and contributes to their purpose in life, they are able to stick to tasks until they achieve the desired outcome.

Their natural talent for self-motivation means that when they need to boost their self-esteem, they are often able to look back on confidence-enhancing success rather than a string of abandoned projects and half-hearted failures.

Developing motivation

Highly motivated people are often very clear what their values are. Consequently, they know what is likely to motivate them to act in most circumstances. Financial security will be important to one person and, hence, a strong motivating factor. This person will ensure that increased financial security is one of the rewards of a proposed course of action. To another person it could have no meaning at all – their values being based on adventure, say, or their standing in the community.

If Nicholas had thought more about his values, he might have been more motivated to continue with the French language course. He's a graphic artist who is very keen on comic strips and graphic novels and feels they deserve more recognition. He hopes to write a book on their early development and now wishes he had the access to the highly regarded French and Belgian *Bande Dessinée* that he would have if he understood the language better.

Look at your values to see where your own motivation lies. Well-motivated people also have other habits of thought that can help you to get motivated and stay motivated.

Get motivated

Optimism, energy and a sense of purpose are an excellent foundation for self-motivation. Setting well-planned personal goals based on your values will help you to keep a sense of purpose – of moving forward and being in control – and maintain an optimistic, positive, upbeat attitude to life.

When you are working in establishing your goals, or planning new ones, remember to build in some motivation for yourself. Do what naturally motivated people do and focus on the benefits and the rewards, build in some feedback, enjoy your future and know how to troubleshoot.

Focus on the benefits and rewards

It's easy to get caught up in anticipating potential problems, hurdles and obstacles when planning objectives. So it's important to take time to imagine, expect and enjoy the positive results of your actions before you start. While you're engaged in your task, take a few minutes every day to visualise, as clearly as you can, the outcome you want, focusing on the end result rather than the details of how to get there. If your goal is a better relationship, for example, visualise having that enjoyable relationship; picture in detail what will be happening when you actually achieve it. Imagine what you are saying, what you are doing and, most importantly, how you are feeling.

Claire often imagined herself talking French in various enjoyable situations – ordering food, chatting to people, and finding her way around interesting backwaters. It helped maintain a feeling of pleasure and excitement, especially when the going got tough.

Build in some feedback

Success is highly motivating. Make sure that you include recognisable points along the route to your goal that will let you know you're getting there, and give you the chance to celebrate.

Claire was thrilled the first time she sent and received an email about booking a room in French. It showed her she was making real progress.

Enjoy your future

Take time to appreciate your future and to link it to your present and your past. Take time once a week or so to review your life; imagine you had an overview. Stand aside from it or float above it and view it as a whole, focusing on the positive things. Notice the paths that lead to where you are today, and appreciate all the positive things that surround you in the present. Notice the pleasant, positive achievements that await you in the future and understand how and where the activities you are embarked on at the moment fit in with your life and form bridges to the future. Appreciate the things you can look forward to and some more if you wish.

Troubleshooting

If you're having trouble getting up the motivation to embark on a task or project, or you keep putting it off or are having difficulty getting started, check it against your values and your roles. Is it something you really want to do, or just something you feel you ought to do? Is it something you really want to do, or is it just a reaction against something else you 'should' or 'ought' to be doing instead? And does it interfere with another goal you have? It might run counter to it, or use up time you need to spend on it.

Charles was having great difficulty getting his neglected, over-grown garden into shape. He wasn't a gardener and had little interest in plants but felt that he ought to make the effort. His real interest was cooking and entertaining friends and he resented having to mow the lawn instead. It occurred to him, however, that he could redesign the garden so that it could be used for barbecues and summer dinner parties. He was quite excited about the idea and with this motivation he soon got everything sorted out.

To get moving on achieving your goal:

- Make it a high priority (see page 20).

- Break it down into smaller steps until you have a first step you can complete in one operation (see page 18).

- Plan some extra reward for yourself for doing it.

Stay motivated

It's easy to stay motivated when things are going well and the rewards are easy to see. It's less easy when you've had a set-back or your goals seem too far away.

Naturally self-motivated people have a number of tricks to help them overcome obstacles. Try some of them when you encounter set-backs.

Do it for 5 minutes. When a task seems too difficult, too big or too boring, promise yourself that you'll do it for just 5 minutes (10 minutes if you can bear it) every day. Keep your promise: do it for exactly 5 minutes and then stop. Either you'll chip away at the task in 5-minute bites until the worst is over, or you'll discover during that 5 minutes that it's not so bad after all.

Do something practical. If things seem slow, pep yourself up by doing something with an immediate, definite result where you can see an instant reward for your labour. Cleaning the car, painting a room, turning out the cupboards and clearing out the garage are all popular ones.

Do something different. When the set-backs seem impassable and the obstacles insurmountable, consider doing something totally off the wall and unpredictable. Try a wild idea, back a wild hunch – or at least give yourself the freedom to imagine what would happen if you did.

Recall the benefits and rewards. Remind yourself what you will gain by carrying on. Make sure you give yourself time to think about, visualise, anticipate and fully appreciate the outcome you are working for.

Get inspired. Keep small things, souvenirs or a scrapbook, that remind you of past pleasures and personal achievements. Dip into it often. Read about people with a strong sense of purpose or those who have overcome challenges. Find quotes, cuttings and anecdotes that have meaning for you and make a scrapbook from them. Succeed at something else. If your motivation is low because of a recent failure, build up your confidence again by doing something you *know* you do well.

Get some support. Make it a life-long project to find people who can encourage you, listen to you and give you practical help or information. Talk through plans, share your dreams, celebrate your successes and bemoan your failures with them. The secret is to spread the load – don't burden one person with all your problems, and remember to return the favour.

Learn from your past. What has motivated you in the past? Popular stimuli that get people moving in the short term include: competition, praise, guilt, treats, discomfort, self-respect, stern lectures, altruism, fear, affirmations, revenge, curiosity, shame, reading about it, starting a group, doing a class, being dared, obstinacy, pride, peer pressure. What has worked for you? Make use of anything that has had a positive result to help remotivate you now.

Learn from the present. What can you learn from the current situation that will be of use to you in the future? What are the positive factors that you can concentrate on? Often, focusing on the positive is all that's needed to rekindle enthusiasm.

Think about the future. What are you looking forward to? What will you enjoy about the next stage of your task or project? Think about what happens after you have got through this difficult part. After a set-back, you sometimes need something quick to re-motivate you and get you going again.

If you need just that little extra to kick-start you into action again, give yourself a holiday. Decide what you need to do next, set a time or date on which you will do it, then give yourself a holiday until that time arrives. Whether it's 10 minutes, 10 days or 10 weeks, take the pressure off and give yourself a complete break during that time.

Troubleshooting checklist

Sometimes you can lose motivation for no apparent reason. If you seem to be losing interest in the goals that you've chosen, consider the following points to put yourself back on track:

- Check your values. Are you drifting out of line or off-target with your goal? Does it really reflect your values? Will it aid your purpose?

- Check your roles. Things change: is your goal based on a role you no longer have?

- Check your goals. Do you still want to achieve it? Or is it something you've outgrown, or satisfied through other means?

- Is the goal challenging enough? If its isn't, upgrade it or move on to something else.

- Is it too challenging? Break it down into easier steps.

- Are your standards too high? Perfectionism can get in the way of achievement. Getting it done is often more important than getting it perfect.

- Are you getting negative messages? Do you feel you're getting disapproval, criticism or lack of interest from people around you? Negative messages can be very demotivating. Give your detractors the benefit of the doubt and put a generous interpretation on what they say (see chapter two, Optimism). Reward and congratulate yourself for what you have achieved so far, and enlist some better support for the future.

- Is something missing? Are there obstacles that could be resolved through practical means? Are there skills or resources that would make things easier? It's surprising how a small practical change can make a big difference.

Recap

Positive thinkers have motivation. Enhance your natural motivation:

- Look at your values to understand what motivates and rewards you.

- Build those rewards into your undertakings.

- Focus on the benefits you will gain from your chosen course of action.

- Anticipate and enjoy those rewards fully.

- Build in feedback to chart your progress towards your goal.

- Have some remotivating tricks up your sleeve in case of set-backs.

5 Realism

Positive thinking is sometimes dismissed as just wishful thinking. True positive thinkers, however, are a very long way from being fantasists. Their positive outlook largely relies on their skills of seeing the world as it is and acting accordingly, rather than imagining it as either far better or much, much worse than reality suggests.

Diane was very nervous about giving her first presentation at work. Her partner told her not to worry, that it would be easy – just throw a few ideas together and do some PowerPoint slides and she'd be fine. People never listened to presentations anyway.

Diane, however, was a realist who preferred to do things her own way. She conquered her nerves by preparing thoroughly and sourcing the best material to illustrate her talk. Far from not listening, the head of the company personally congratulated her and Diane went on to give many more presentations, her confidence and professionalism growing with each one.

Why is realism useful?

Far from believing that everything will work out all right if you just wish it to, or that anybody can do everything without effort or application, people who naturally think positively understand that it takes time to build up a skill or a reputation and it takes effort to learn something, create something and build something. They know that it takes determination to see things through and it takes patience to see results. They fully appreciate, moreover, that luck mostly happens to people who have already done the groundwork, and that this is an imperfect world and you can't count on magic.

They remain positive and optimistic not only despite these realisations, but to some extent because of them. With that understanding, they undertake new tasks and projects with a full realisation of what they need to put into them, and consequently avoid being disappointed, frustrated or running out of steam halfway through. They appreciate that most success must be earned and they can go into things without holding back for fear of failure and are willing to try new things without expecting to get it right first time. They put in time and effort to get results and undertake things without expecting perfection.

Realism is what stops positive thinkers from turning into fantasists with rose-tinted spectacles. They have a certain toughness and willingness to take the rough with the smooth.

Developing the skill of realism means they are not afraid to wade in and have a go at things – if they fail, then that's just life and no great tragedy. They rarely see it as failure, though. They focus instead on what they've got right and what they could do differently another time. They learn from the situation.

Realists have the optimism, self-motivation and courage to appreciate that one of the easiest ways to deal with difficulties is to tackle them and get them out of the way as quickly as possible. Without dwelling on the negative, they have a philosophical acceptance of the way the world is, and realise that life is much simpler when you face up to problems and get the boring or difficult stuff out of the way first. They accept that there are things they're responsible for, so they are, for the most part, able to stop putting things off and hoping they'll just go away.

Developing realism

Optimism, energy, purpose and self-motivation are an excellent foundation from which to face the realities of life. To develop that resilient, optimistic realism that characterises natural positive thinkers, copy some of the habits of natural realists, and recognise your mistakes, take risks, focus on doing rather than dreaming, and be honest with yourself.

Recognise your mistakes

Everybody has times when they could have done better, but blaming yourself only undermines your confidence and self-esteem, and makes it harder to try again. Accept that everybody, including you, makes mistakes. Looking at them in a positive light and learning from them puts you in a stronger, more positive position than just trying to avoid any situation where you might make mistakes in future.

Lawrence missed a deadline by not sending in a report on time. He could have been pessimistic and negative about it: 'This always happens to me, I can't even get anything right. I'm not right for this job. I can't cope with the demands.' He could on the other hand, have taken an overly rose-tinted view: 'It'll be all right, they won't mind. It wasn't that important anyway.' Both would have been equally unrealistic.

Lawrence's realistic view was: 'It would have been on time if the printer had been working properly. I noticed there was something wrong last week and did nothing about it. I do have a tendency to put things off or leave them until the last moment. I left the details to chance, and then ran into difficulties. I won't do it again.'

By being open-minded and realistic about a situation, you can recognise and accept how a problem has come about. You will then be in a strong position to do something positive and practical about it, so there will be fewer similar mistakes in future. In recognising your mistakes, you can replace your bad habits with positive ones.

First, decide what you want to change. Work out what's at the root of the problem. In the example above, it's the habit of putting things off until they become urgent. Then decide what you want to do instead: replace your negative habit with a positive one. Decide what you would rather do and state it clearly to yourself. Keep it positive – focus on what you want to do rather than what you *don't* want to do. In the above example it could be: 'I want to take positive action on problems as they arise.'

Now you need to look for opportunities to make this change. Think about how you are actually going to behave in similar situations in the future. Rehearse it in your imagination and plan what you are going to do. Try it out – be alert for chances to put your new habit into practice. What happens when you do this? Are there ways you could improve it? Are there times when you slip back into the old habit? How can you get over that? And finally, reward yourself. Give yourself a small reward and lots of praise and encouragement whenever you use your new habit. Avoid punishing or scolding yourself if you make a mistake; just remind yourself you could do it better next time.

Take risks

Failure is not the end of the world. Positive thinkers have their steady optimism to pull them through difficulties but, as realists, they also recognise that there are no guarantees in life and you sometimes have to risk failing in order to succeed. While it is tempting to seek comfort and certainty, we need some challenge in order to test our own strength and realise our own potential.

Being adventurous is stimulating, it builds self-esteem and self-reliance and seems to account for much of the 'stress hardiness' of positive thinkers. Interestingly, in the long term it seems to make little difference whether the outcome is successful or not. It's actually *taking* the risk that's important, rather than ducking out or waiting for the soft option.

Risk doing what you enjoy

Do things that you enjoy for their own sake; don't worry about success or failure. Risk not being good at what you do; just bring commitment and enthusiasm to it. Do something that you can lose yourself in without being conscious of mistakes or shortcomings.

Try something new

Taking risks, being adventurous and doing something new all stimulate self-confidence. Attempting something that you have never tried before enhances belief in your self and your abilities, and helps build up your resources. Here are some suggestions:

- Book a holiday somewhere unusual but tempting.

- Do a class in something you've never done but might enjoy.

- Go on a course you think you'll find interesting.

- Write a letter to a national magazine or newspaper.

- Ring up an acquaintance you'd like to know better.

- Pick up a 'difficult' book and just plough through it.

- Volunteer for something at work.

- Write a short article and send it to your local paper.

- Join a new club or society.

- Try a type of food you've never eaten before.

- Try a difficult recipe.

- Take another route to work.

- Enrol on an activity holiday you've always wanted to do.

- Book the test, enrol for the exam or try for that qualification you've always put off doing.

- Enter a competition.

- Try a new sport.

Don't just dream, do

Realists recognise that one action is worth a thousand words. While imagining positive outcomes and planning are important first steps, realists understand that in order to achieve anything, above all, they have to *do*. Whatever your goals, take persistent, regular steps, however small, towards completing them. Do something every day, however little, however hard it is.

When Maggie wrote her first novel she was still working full time and had a family to look after. She felt, though, that if she didn't write about the characters whirling around in her head she would go mad. She reckoned that she could find an hour every evening to write and instead of driving to work she started to take the train so that she could spend the morning journey editing the previous night's work, and the journey home making notes and preparing.

Although it seemed impossibly daunting to begin with, Maggie quickly fell into a routine and was surprised and delighted by the way even one hour's writing began to mount up over the weeks and months. She realised the importance of just doing it – you actually have to perform the tasks and activities required to reach your goal.

Realistically assess the amount of effort that you will need to put into your own goal and decide if you have the time, self-motivation and enthusiasm necessary. If you decide to go ahead, don't agonise about waiting for the right time, or put it off until you get into the right mood, *just do it*.

Be honest with yourself

Realists are very honest with themselves. They know themselves well, they value themselves, and they accept that their happiness and well-being are ultimately their own responsibility. They acknowledge their mistakes and make amends for them. They know when they're in the wrong and apologise fully and generously. They understand when they are living at odds with their own values and are quick to put things right. They also recognise and accept the difference between reasons and excuses. We all make excuses: 'I'm too tired', 'I haven't got the time', and so on. Even when there are things that we really want to do the effort can seem too much and it's easier to make an excuse rather than work out how we can do it. Realists rarely allow themselves to hide behind an excuse, they prefer to come up with practical ideas and strategies about how to overcome the problem.

Let the following examples inspire you to copy their approach.

Excuse: 'I've got too much else to do'
Strategy:

- Check your commitments: are you taking on too many roles?

- Do they *all* fit in with your values?

- Enlist help, explain what you are aiming to do and ask for practical support.

- Work out your priorities. Is what you want to do more important or less important than the things you are already doing?

Excuse: 'I haven't got the time'
Strategy:

- Work expands (and contracts) to fill the time available. Is there something you could 'borrow' time from?

- Work out what you have got time for and do that bit, however little.

- Plan out a timetable to make the best use of your time.

- Budget your time like money: find out what you spend it on, where could you make savings and where could you invest more.

Excuse: 'I haven't got the confidence'
Strategy:

- Nor has anyone else – confidence can only be built up gradually through doing things and learning from mistakes.

- See chapter eight, the comfort trap (page 102).

Excuse: 'I'm too tired to do it'
Strategy:

- Check your health – see chapter three, energy (page 35).

- Exercise more – paradoxically, it could help you to feel less tired.

- Are you tired, or just uninspired? Boredom can feel very much like tiredness.

- If you feel you suffer from more than ordinary levels of tiredness, check with your GP.

Excuse: 'I'm not sure it's what I want'
Strategy:

- Check your values and your purpose in life to see how and where it fits in.

- Work out the worst that could happen if you do it, work out how you would recover from it and decide if it's a risk worth taking.

- See chapter seven, indecision (page 92).

Excuse: 'What would people say about it?'
Strategy:

- Are the people involved significant people in your life or just generalised, nebulous 'other people'?

- Find out what those significant people think by talking it over with them.

- Work out the worst that could happen if significant people disapprove of what you do, work out how you would deal with it and then decide if the risk is worth taking.

Realists are also honest enough themselves to admit that, sometimes, whatever the reasons, whatever the excuses, there are some things that they just don't *want* to do.

Recap

Positive thinkers have realism. Enhance your natural realism:

- Accept that things are not always easy, but that doesn't mean that they're invariably dreadful.

- Admit that you make mistakes, and learn from them.

- Recognise bad habits and replace them with positive ones.

- Accept that doing new things is a risk.

- Take small, regular steps towards the things you want even when it's hard.

- Be honest with yourself and don't put up with excuses.

Part two

Conquering gremlins

In part one of this book, we looked at the positive beliefs, attitudes and behaviours that are characteristic of positive thinkers, how these contribute considerably to the way they approach life and get the most out of it, and how you can emulate them with similar satisfying results.

That's fine, you may be thinking, when life is running smoothly. But what happens when things go wrong? We may have little say in some of the things that happen to us, but we can nearly always choose how we respond to them. Positive thinkers aren't immune from having bad things happen to them, but they cope better and respond more constructively when they do. They have strategies for dealing with the underlying factors that colour their responses to adversity, so that they are free to tackle problems positively and assertively.

This part of the book takes a positive look at how you can deal with gremlins – those niggling, negative thoughts, beliefs and attitudes that can sometimes get in the way of living positively. There are some fundamental ways of thinking and behaving that are the root cause of the negative responses we sometimes find ourselves making in certain circumstances. They are:

- negativity

- indecision

- the comfort trap

- hurry sickness

- demand thinking

- making comparisons.

By understanding and adopting the sort of tactics that positive thinkers employ, you can overcome these things and develop more vigorous approaches to problems. The following chapters give practical advice and guidance on what these various gremlins are, how they arise, and how you can develop ways of overcoming them that suit your own individual circumstances.

Let's start by conquering negativity.

6 Negativity

Negativity is the sum total of those negative thoughts, feelings and beliefs that we all have to a greater or lesser extent.

Individually, each thought or feeling would be easy to deal with. However, sometimes we can get caught in a downward spiral where negative thoughts breed negative feelings, which give rise to negative behaviour. The negative feedback we get from the negative behaviour creates more negative thoughts and feelings, and so it goes on.

Why negativity happens and how to overcome it

We get a lot of negative messages from the world, especially while we are growing up. Parents, teachers, siblings, peers, they all have an effect on us, and we learn early on that life can be a risky, dangerous and disappointing business. We get plenty of negative messages, such as: don't expect too much, pride comes before a fall, don't count your chickens before they are hatched, never rest on your laurels, you must always try harder, you'll be sorry, the higher you fly the harder you fall, those that don't ask don't get, don't invite disappointment.

They were meant to be helpful but they often left us with the impression, from an early age, that the world is a grudging, capricious, mean-spirited place. The results can be lingering feelings of guilt and unease, a sense of foreboding, and a deep suspicion of doing or saying anything that might tempt fate.

These negative messages can have far-reaching effects. When Isla was little her parents, with the best of intentions, kept giving her well-meaning advice about the way she played with other children. They naturally wanted her to be liked and have lots of friends but what they kept saying was, 'People won't like you if you're selfish', 'People won't like you if you're too rough', in the hope that they were teaching her good friendship skills.

They meant well, and they did teach their daughter to be unselfish, gentle and caring, but the message that really got through to Isla was, 'People won't like you.' Not surprisingly, she grew up thinking not only that she was unlikable, but that she could only be likable if she behaved perfectly all the time, never getting angry or impatient or despondent, which she found impossible.

Consequently, she became shy and uncertain about getting close to others and had few friends. People thought she was a nice person, but rarely felt they knew the real Isla. Isla had to work hard to change this negative belief – to see herself as a fundamentally likeable person and stop listening to the negative little voice in her imagination that kept insisting, 'People won't like you.'

There are three keys to overcoming negativity. You need to build up a positive image of yourself and the world around you, change the negative voice inside your head into a positive one and challenge negative feelings with positive ones.

Build a positive image

Your image of yourself is largely based on your perception of your individual skills and qualities – what you are, what you do, and how well (or badly) you believe you do it.

Positive people have a very clear idea of what their skills and qualities are. This helps them maintain their self-respect and self-esteem, and gives them a realistic, practical foundation for their goals and purpose in life. They also have a clear, realistic idea of what their strengths and weaknesses are. They are able to recognise, appreciate and use their strengths, and take steps to correct or modify weaknesses where these may be a hindrance.

David believed he had the talent to become a full-time artist. His work sold well at local exhibitions and was admired by fellow painters but he was still hesitant. He knew he had the technical skill and the creative drive necessary and was keen to develop these further. But he also knew that turning professional meant contacting galleries and talking to people who he felt could be very intimidating. Rather than dismissing the idea completely because of this weakness, David found a course on presentation skills. Although it was meant more for business people than artists, it showed him how other people coped with the same problems and gave him enough of the skills he needed to increase his confidence.

Build a positive, realistic picture of yourself. Look at your skills, your qualities, your strengths and your weaknesses.

Skills

Your skills are the knowledge and ability that you have acquired and developed over the years. Some skills will be highly practical

– typing, driving, and book-keeping, for example. Others will be more abstract and intuitive – communicating, negotiating or motivating.

Some skills, perhaps the ones you use at work, will be more highly developed than others, but everyone has a range of skills – some with people, some with things, others with ideas. Everything you do uses some mixture of skills. This can be at work, at home, with family, as a partner, as a parent, studying, pursuing interests, pursuing hobbies, pursuing concerns, doing sports, doing crafts, for fun, with friends, or on your own.

People who are natural positive thinkers often place a high value on all their skills. They see the skills they develop through hobbies such as music or sport, or a role such as parenting, as being just as important as those developed for work. This gives them a wide range of opportunities to consciously exercise and develop their skills and talents, with the accompanying lift to their self-esteem that might be expected.

To develop your positive image of yourself, look at your own skills. What are your abilities? Think about all the things you do, and all the different skills you use. Some examples to start you thinking are: organising, making, delegating, communicating, presenting, studying, repairing, specifying, listening, driving, crafting, managing, planning, innovating, computing, typing, leading, building, writing, counselling, teaching, accounting, budgeting, campaigning, fund-raising, negotiating, motivating, supervising, travelling, creating, observing, reporting, analysing, influencing, selling, trading.

Make a list of all your skills and take the opportunity to reflect on them and enjoy them. Then, looking at each of them in turn, decide whether you want to improve or strengthen it, add to it in any way, use it more often, or that you're happy with it as it is.

Paul made a survey of some of his skills and thought about how he could use them to enhance his life:

SKILL	WHAT TO DO WITH IT
Management	Use more often. Use time management skills to organise leisure time rather than frittering it away on chores. Use negotiating skills with children rather than bossing them around.
Language	Add to – develop spoken and written German for increased business use.
Photography	Improve – apply for course in September, timetable one weekend a month for day out with camera.
Music	Do nothing – just enjoy it as it is.

He listed the things he wanted to do, such as finding a photography class, getting a better camera, planning some days out, finding a German language course, etc. As with planning any other sort of goal you'll need to think about the steps you must take in order to explore or develop your skills.

Qualities

Your qualities are aspects of your character and personality that have developed over a lifetime. Whether you're born with them or acquire them early on, a good self-image depends on recognising, appreciating and strengthening the qualities that we like in ourselves. These can include things such as:

Kindness, intelligence, responsibility, leadership, understanding, friendliness, ambition, dependability, flexibility, versatility, perception, diplomacy, wit, punctuality, imagination, determination, unflappability, efficiency, sensitivity, practicality, honesty, persistence, energy, patience.

Think about which personal qualities you value and are important to you. List your own qualities and enjoy recognising them and appreciating them. Then, as with your skills, look at each of them in turn and decide whether you want to improve or strengthen it, add to it in any way, use it more often, or that you're happy with it as it is.

Paul took this look at his qualities:

QUALITY	WHAT TO DO WITH IT
Versatility	Use more often – try out different ways of doing things instead of relying on the usual approaches.
Assertiveness	Improve – find assertiveness course or self-help book.
Energy	Add to it – improve diet and go to bed earlier. Do one active thing over the weekend.
Patience	Do nothing – content with it as it is.

Make a list of the things that you want to do, then plan the steps needed to carry them out.

Strengths

Strengths are the things that you're good at – the mixture of skills and qualities that you feel confident about using. Write down the things that you do well, and list all the skills and qualities that go with each particular activity.

Laura considered both work and home life when she was thinking about the things she was good at:

I AM GOOD AT	SKILLS NEEDED	QUALITIES NEEDED
Designing and making my own clothes	designing, adapting, planning, budgeting, dress-making	imagination, patience, energy, practicality, aesthetics
Producing the company magazine	desktop publishing, organising, design, communication, negotiation	tact, responsibility, versatility, imagination, wit
Teaching photography	photographic – technical and artistic, teaching, organising communication, listening, motivating	friendliness, discipline, understanding, patience, persistence

Look at your strengths and enjoy them. You can use all these skills and qualities to improve your quality of life and well-being, to have fun and to pursue your life purpose. Are there skills that you could add, or qualities you could develop, that would further enhance your strong points?

Weaknesses

What are the things that let you down and get in the way of your strengths? Note any weaknesses you may have and decide for each whether you want to improve it, you can get around it or compensate for it, or that it's not particularly important.

George is an office manager with excellent communication skills, but he does have a couple of weaknesses that bother him and that he felt needed tackling in some way.

WEAKNESS	WHAT TO DO ABOUT IT
Poor punctuality	Improve it – get alarm clock mended or buy new one. Set watch 5 minutes ahead and use in-built alarm for appointments.
Lack of authority	Compensate – use communication skills and qualities of understanding and patience instead.
Can't drive	Do nothing – it's not that important while I live in the city.

List all the things that you want to do and plan accordingly.

Surround yourself with positivity

As well as working on developing a positive self-image, cultivate positive experiences of the world around you. Find and keep upbeat stories. Ask friends what they enjoy in life, swap stories about the best times you ever had, ask them what's going well at the moment and ask your family too. Read biographies and autobiographies about happy, worthwhile people who have fun occasionally and keep a list of people who have achieved something against the odds and add one name a week to it. Collect cheerful quotes and sayings and pin them up where you can see them and add postcards, pictures, cartoons and photographs that make you smile.

Look positive, be SOFT

Even when you don't feel positive, you can always look positive. It's strange but true that behaving in a positive manner will often make you feel more positive, however you feel when you start. If other people perceive you as most positive, they start to treat you more positively and, with that positive feedback, you actually come to feel more positive yourself.

An easy way to appear positive – confident, friendly and approachable – is suggested by the acronym SOFT. This stands for:

Smile   Smile and look cheerful, and other people will respond to you positively.

Open   Use open rather than closed, defensive postures. Hold your head up and keep your shoulders back. Rest your hands in your lap or on the arm of your chair, rather than folding your arms across your chest.

Forward   Look forward and towards the person you are speaking to; don't back away from them. Face them and make eye contact. Clearly and confidently direct your attention towards them.

Touch   Cultivate a firm, confident handshake for a positive first impression.

Change the negative voice

A lot of us seem to carry a little negative voice around in the back of our minds a lot of the time, criticising and undermining what we do. Maybe it's an echo of the past, or of our own negative experiences, but overcoming negativity means turning that derogatory voice into an encouraging, supportive one. To do that we need to turn negative labels into positive ones and turn negative self-talk into positive self-talk.

Turn negative labels into positive ones

We often put labels on ourselves and our behaviour, and these labels can be quite negative at times: 'I'm terribly bossy', 'I'm just being lazy', 'You must think me awfully silly', and so on.

Positive people think optimistically and give others the benefit of the doubt, putting the best possible interpretation on their behaviour. They are also able to do the same for themselves. They give their 'negative' traits a positive interpretation, and are able to recognise that there are positive sides even to supposedly undesirable characteristics.

Try replacing some of your negative labels with more positive ones. Many supposed faults have a much more favourable description that could help you to focus on your positive qualities.

Someone who's timid, for example, could be more positively described as cautious. Someone else could be considered relaxed and laid-back instead of the more negative lazy.

Nearly every negative label has a more positive interpretation:

NEGATIVE LABEL	POSITIVE LABEL
Old-fashioned	Traditional
Fussy	Attentive to detail
Shy	Sensitive
Aggressive	Determined
Rude	Forthright
Bossy	Responsible
Stuffy	Formal
Loud	Enthusiastic

Thinking about yourself positively and generously helps you to work with your character and develop your potential. If you've labelled yourself as stubborn, for example, you may see this as negative and try to play it down. But by doing so, you may notice that this characteristic is also what encourages you to be persistent and to keep going in the face of set-backs.

Changing the way you label yourself from 'stubborn' to 'persistent' allows you to express the positive aspect of your natural tenacity, while also opening the door to greater flexibility in your behaviour.

Turn negative self-talk into positive self-talk

Stop the self-critical talk that we all indulge in at times. We are often our own harshest critics, but frequent criticism saps self-confidence and makes it difficult to feel either optimistic or positive.

When you catch yourself making negative judgments about yourself or your performance, stop and think what the generous interpretation would be. Replacing negative comments with more positive ones allows you to, optimistically and realistically, learn from experience and try again.

Most negative statements can be turned into neutral observations of the actual facts at least. For example, instead of telling yourself: 'I did something terrible', just state the facts: 'I made a mistake'. Mistakes can be rectified and avoided another time. There's more chance that you'll do better next time if you tell yourself that you simply made a mistake than if you tell yourself you did something terrible. When you catch yourself out with a negative statement, consciously turn it into a positive one:

NEGATIVE STATEMENT	POSITIVE STATEMENT
I did something terrible	I made a mistake
I'm no good	I'm OK
I can't do this	This will take time and concentration
They won't like me	They'll probably think I'm OK
I must do better	I could improve by doing it differently
I'm a clumsy idiot	I just tripped over
I ought to try harder	I'm doing well in the circumstances

Avoid negative experiences

Where possible, avoid situations that you know are going to be negative unless you have very clear reasons for staying. In particular, avoid indulging in:

- negative conversations – backbiting, complaining, etc.
- doom, gloom and despair in the news
- people who want to criticise everything
- people who want you to share their feeling of helplessness
- people who want to compete for the worst thing that happened to them
- people who want you to share their bad health habits
- biographies and autobiographies about miserable, desperate people who never have fun
- people who always run other people down
- miserable songs
- depressing stories, plays and films about people without hope.

Challenge negative feelings with their opposites

We all have negative feelings at times and, surprisingly, negative feelings are quite useful. When they arise naturally and appropriately, they tell us when something in our world is not as it should be and needs attention. Fear, for example, primes us for fight or flight when we are threatened. Anger alerts us that something unjust or unfair is happening.

The primary negative feelings are fear, grief, jealousy or envy, and anger.

Problems arise when these valuable signals linger on past their usefulness. Anger settles down into habitual bad temper or aggression, fear becomes the established response to any and every situation, grief dwindles into apathy and disillusionment. Rather than letting them take root, combat persistent negative feelings with their opposite, positive feeling: courage, cheerfulness, self-esteem and assertiveness. Balancing negative emotions with positive ones allows you to retain a sense of realism and perspective. Let's look at some of these useful positive/negative emotional balances.

Courage and fear

The good news about fear is it is natural, useful and can be controlled. Fear is the unavoidable consequence of having a nervous system designed to keep us safe and out of danger. It alerts us to danger and gets our bodies ready for fight or flight – increased heart rate, rapid breathing, and so on. Courage isn't the absence of fear, it just means overcoming the fear and either tackling the cause of alarm or carrying on despite it, whichever is appropriate. Here are some positive steps you can take to develop your natural courage.

Tackle the source of your fears. When you relax and look at your fears realistically and objectively, is there some foundation to them? Are there practical things you could do to alleviate them? You may, for example, be right to fear public speaking if you've had no training and very little practice at it, and sensible to worry about burglars if your home has proved insecure in the past. Practical remedies to both these problems are readily apparent.

Change the voice in your head. Adopt a positive attitude. Instead of telling yourself: 'This is frightening', 'I'm too scared', 'I can't do this', etc., use positive statements like 'This is challenging', 'I'm excited', 'Adrenaline improves my performance', 'This is an adventure', 'I'm alert and in control here'.

Tackle fears step by step. Start with the easiest, least frightening things and work your way up. Remember to reward yourself every time you accomplish something new.

Cheerfulness and grief

Grief is a painful but inevitable part of a full life. Naturally positive people learn to deal with it sensitively and fittingly, rather than trying to avoid it and thereby restricting their lives unreasonably. They realise that grief is an entirely natural reaction to loss. The grief we feel when something is gone is in proportion to its value and importance to us. To go through life without ever grieving would be to go through life without ever valuing anything, or thinking anything important.

Grief is healing from the wound, not the wound itself. The pain will heal more quickly and thoroughly if grief is allowed its full expression through tears, talking about the loss, remembering and mourning. Grief has a beginning, a middle and – although it may not seem like it at the time – an end. Grief becomes a negative rather than a healing force when, for whatever reason, the process becomes stuck and we can't move on beyond it.

Near the end of the grieving process, a time comes when it is natural and appropriate for cheerfulness to start springing up again. Never feel that you have to cling on to unhappiness for any reason. Even if you don't quite feel like it, give laughter at least an opportunity to break in on a regular basis:

• Search out comedy programmes on television and radio.

• Borrow 'comedy classic' DVDs from the library.

• Choose light-hearted films rather than serious ones.

• Read books and magazines you find funny.

- See people who you know you can have a laugh with.

- Do things that are fun and make you laugh.

- Listen to upbeat music during the day – even if it's not the sort of thing you would usually listen to, try to lift your spirits.

Self-esteem and envy

Few of us have everything we want or secretly think we deserve and seeing others succeed can spark off feelings that have their roots deep in infancy, when getting what we needed was, quite literally, a matter of life or death. Envy is useful – it can be a clear signal about what we want in our lives – you only envy in others what you value in yourself. If you use envy as the spur to making positive, productive changes in your own life, then a touch of it can prove useful. It becomes very negative, however, when it turns to unproductive brooding and resentment of others.

Avoid the negative envy trap by building a solid foundation of self-esteem – turn negative talk into positive talk. If you set and achieve goals that are meaningful to you in the light of your values and purpose, then you need never envy anyone anything.

Assertiveness and anger

There are even positive aspects to anger. The energy of anger, properly handled, can be channelled into productive activity to improve the situation. If you want to achieve mastery over it, you need to learn how to channel the anger and develop your assertiveness:

Relax. Take time regularly to relax both physically and mentally, to keep yourself calm (see chapter three, energy, page 35).

Tackle the source of your anger. Where anger is the signal that something is wrong, look at what is making you angry realistically and objectively. Is there something practical you can do about it?

Change the voice in your head. Instead of telling yourself, 'This is unbearable', use positive statements like 'I can keep calm and deal with this'.

Release it. This can be physical, through:

- Strenuous exercise – running, swimming, aerobics, anything vigorous.

- Competitive sport – team games can provide a regular outlet.

- Hard physical labour – digging the garden, scrubbing floors, chopping wood, sawing logs.

- Shouting – choose somewhere harmless, or shout into a pillow.

- Pillow punching, which can be combined with shouting.

The release can also be emotional. It helps to write things down – so try writing letters, in which you can express your grievances fully and comprehensively, getting all your anger and hurt out on to the paper. These letters are not for sending to anyone so you can say whatever you like. Remember to destroy them afterwards, though! You could also make a list of all the things you feel angry about. You might write, for example: I am angry with the children for being naughty, I am angry with Tony because he wouldn't take me seriously. When you've finished, look back over your list and decide what you would rather have happened in each case. This helps you to think more calmly about what has actually made you angry. For example: I would have preferred the children to be quiet and reasonable, I would have preferred Tony to have listened to me seriously. Is there anything you can do, now that you're calm rather than angry, that would change the situation? Would talking to the person involved, for example, help them to understand why you are angry? Could you negotiate anything different in the future? Could you behave differently?

Decide on your rights. Think about the situations where you tend to get angry, and write a list of the things that you feel nobody has the right to do to you. You might decide, for example, that: nobody has the right to tell me what to do, nobody has the right to treat me as second rate, nobody has the right to ignore me. Look back over your list and decide what this means that you have the right to, in positive terms. Given the list above, for example, you might decide that: I have a right to my independence, I have a right to be taken seriously, I have a right to be treated well. This might help you to see the root of your resentment more clearly, and to understand where your self-esteem might be under threat. You can then begin to think clearly about how to change things.

If you'd rather not write things down, try talking it over with someone. Choose someone who you think will listen to you without interrupting or telling you what to do. Ask them first if they are willing to listen, but don't be hurt if they say they can't; some people do find it very difficult. Just ask someone else.

Laughter can release both the physical and the emotional tension of anger and restore your sense of perspective. Take all the opportunities you can to laugh. Watch comedy programmes on television, spend time with people who can let go and be silly, play with children, read books and magazines you find funny.

Recap

To help yourself to overcome negativity:

- Develop your self-esteem:
  - know what your skills and qualities are
  - develop them further
  - understand your strengths and work with them
  - understand and deal with your weaknesses.

- Change your negative labels into positive ones.
- Cut out the negative self-talk.
- Pursue positive experiences and avoid negative ones.
- Understand your negative emotions and learn to channel them positively. Counter:
  - fear with courage
  - grief with cheerfulness
  - jealousy with self-esteem
  - anger with assertiveness.

7 Indecision

People who are natural positive thinkers are, on the whole, clear and decisive about what they want to do and what they want to happen. This is a natural result of their sense of purpose and optimism.

However, even the most confident, assertive, positive people can be familiar with indecision. Sometimes it's hard to be decisive about what to have for lunch, let alone long-term goals. Usually though, the bigger the impact the decision will have, the harder it is to reach it. It can sometimes seem easier to just let things take their own course and hope for the best.

Indecision usually happens when you have to choose between two or more options and can't because all the options look equally attractive or unattractive. Sometimes, you may make a choice but keep changing your mind about it, or you make a choice but, for some reason, you're reluctant to put it into effect. Sometimes, you can't make a choice because there don't seem to be any options to choose from or the option you'd like isn't open to you, so you have to choose between 'second-best' options. And sometimes, you didn't realise you had a choice so didn't explore any other options until it was too late.

Why does indecision happen?

Indecision is often linked to a lack of purpose. If you have no clear direction and little sense of what you want your future to be, then making decisions can be very hard.

Jack found it extremely difficult to decide which university course to do. He had a talent for maths but was more interested in subjects like history and geography that dealt with people. He had no clear idea about what sort of work he ultimately wanted to do or what sort of life he wanted.

In the end Jack decided to do computer sciences because he thought it might lead to a good job, but once he started the course he found it unsatisfying. In his second year he changed to psychology, which he found interesting as a subject but he kept asking himself what he was going to do with it as he didn't see himself actually working as a psychologist. Because his heart wasn't in it, Jack ended up with a much poorer degree than he deserved and left university still unsure of what he was going to do. It took several years and a further course of training before he began to find a niche for himself as a teacher where his talent for maths, interest in people and knowledge of psychology all started to work together for him rather than dragging him in different directions.

Sometimes, lack of realism can lead to feelings of either hopeless pessimism – 'It doesn't matter what I want, things never go right for me anyway' – or rose-tinted false optimism – 'Why choose? Things will work out all right somehow, they always do.'

Even with purpose and realism, though, decision-making can still be difficult. There are all sorts of reasons why indecision can subconsciously appear to be, at least in the short term, the easier option.

A key factor is fear. Making a decision about something can bring up various fears:

- fear of failure – of not making the right choice

- fear of commitment – of having to say goodbye to all the other options

- fear of getting it wrong – classic procrastination, putting off a decision while gathering more and yet more data

- fear of criticism – of making a choice that others will disapprove of.

Rescue fantasies are manifestations of another type of fear – fear of responsibility. The feeling that it would be much better if someone else would make the decision, or make the need to decide unnecessary, can be very tempting. It can also breed feelings of resentment when no such rescue materialises.

Perfectionism, the idea that there is only one right way to do something, and that you somehow have to work out what that is, is very inhibiting. And this is made worse by a lack of practice. Young people particularly, but older ones too, sometimes get very little practice in making their own decisions and in assessing and choosing their own options. Somebody else usually does it for them, especially when it comes to major events. Suddenly finding their future in their own hands can be very daunting.

And sometimes you know exactly what you should do, but just don't want to do it. This can disguise itself as indecision and feel just as uncomfortable as the real thing.

Why is indecision a problem?

Many people never get around to making decisions about their lives just because of those uncomfortable feelings of fear. Unhappily, any natural sense of purpose soon gets lost in the subsequent random drift of events. Optimism may be swallowed up in feelings of frustration and futility, energy without direction can turn destructively inwards, and it is rarely possible to remain motivated by choices in which you have little faith.

It's difficult to feel positive regarding a future about which you've made few choices, and over which you feel you have little or no control. While there is no foolproof way of unerringly making the right choice, greater confidence in decision-making can lead to increased autonomy and a more positive attitude.

The natural realism of positive people accepts that not all decisions turn out perfectly. You can never foresee all the consequences and you will never have all the data you need. You will sometimes change your mind and not always for logical reasons. But positive people also know that even bad decisions can turn out well sometimes.

Overcoming indecision

You need to build on your natural decisiveness and determination. Follow the advice in part one and get a clear picture of yourself and your purpose in life – where you're going and what you're doing. Understand your values and, consequently, what motivates you, and also make sure tiredness and stress aren't the root cause of your hesitancy. Look at what's positive and interesting about opportunities before focusing on what is negative, then look for solutions rather than dwelling on the problem. Be realistic about how much you are prepared to put into any situation but be prepared to risk trying something new. Above all, be honest with yourself about the source of your indecision.

The decision-making process

If you are still having trouble reaching a decision about something, try going through this structured decision-making process based on your values, to select the option that's right for you.

List all your options

Take time to think about this stage and put down *all* the possibilities, not just the most obvious ones, the ones you feel you ought to do, or the first ones that come to mind.

Paula has had a job as a designer for a prestigious company for four years. She is ambitious and anxious to move ahead and a position in management has arisen. She stands an excellent chance of getting it – should she apply for the post?

Her most obvious options are either to stay in the same position or to apply for the management job. But thinking about it further, she came up with some more options. She could apply for a different design job, go back to college to undertake further study, or set up her own business.

List your values and put them in order

Take the values that you listed in chapter one (see page 3). Put them in order of importance to you and give each value points according to its position. If you have ten values, for example, give your top value ten points, your next highest nine points, and so on down to your lowest value which will have only one point.

Paula's values are freedom, creativity, challenge, variety, innovation, simplicity and independence. Her most important value is creativity so she puts this at the top of the list and gives it seven points (as she has seven values). Next, she puts independence with six points, and so on down the list.

VALUE	POINTS
Creativity	7
Independence	6
Innovation	5
Variety	4
Challenge	3
Freedom	2
Simplicity	1

Compare each option with your values

Alongside each option, list each value that it satisfies together with the number of points you have given it. Add up the total points. The highest scoring options will be the ones that most clearly suit your own personal values.

Paula did this with her options:

OPTION	VALUES SATISFIED	POINTS	TOTAL
Stay in same job	Creativity	7	
	Variety	4	
	Challenge	3	
	Simplicity	1	15
Apply for management job	Challenge	3	
	Variety	4	
	Innovation	5	12
Apply for another design job	Creativity	7	
	Variety	4	
	Challenge	3	14
Go back to college	Creativity	7	
	Challenge	3	
	Innovation	5	
	Freedom	2	
	Variety	4	21
Set up own business	Creativity	7	
	Challenge	3	
	Innovation	5	
	Variety	4	
	Independence	6	25

Applying for the manager's job fulfils only lower-scoring values and achieves the lowest total of 12. Clearly, a move into management would not be in Paula's interests. If her values had been different, though, the result would have been different too. Had her top values been money, security and prestige, for instance, her best options might well have included applying for the management job.

From her original options – stay in the same job or apply for the new post – staying in her present job would suit her better than applying for the management job. Going back to college or setting up her own design business, however, would be even better choices.

List the drawbacks

List the downsides to the top two or three options. This may seem rather negative and not at all the sort of thing a positive thinker should be doing, but realistically acknowledging the drawbacks pulls them out into the open and helps to start the process of looking for solutions – a very positive activity.

Paula's best options, for example, are either going back to college or starting her own business. She assesses the drawbacks of each course of action:

OPTION	DRAWBACKS
Going back to college	Lack of money Finding new job after training
Starting own design business	Financial insecurity High workload Stress Learning business skills

List the solutions

Once you have the drawbacks in front of you, apply solution-focused optimism to finding ways to counter them.

Even if, by this stage, you feel a clear winner is emerging, it can still be a positive activity to list all your solutions for all your options.

This way, you will be definitely be choosing the option that suits you best rather than just avoiding the option that seems to have most problems.

When you know that you could, if you wanted, select any of your options, you can genuinely make a free decision about the one that you want.

Paula's solutions looked like this:

OPTION	DRAWBACKS	SOLUTIONS
Going back to college	Lack of money	Save hard for next six months Find freelance projects
	Find new job after training	Use college course as springboard for networking
Starting own design business	Financial insecurity High workload	Plan, budget, save Budget time efficiently Drop inessentials during start-up phase Consider setting up with someone else
	Stress Learning business skills	Learn to relax Find short, practical course about self-employment

Paula can now make an absolutely free choice about what she wants to do with her future. In the end, she decides that going back to college to continue her specialised training to a higher level will be the most satisfying option. It fulfils many of her highest priority values – creativity, freedom and challenge, and she sees it offering her a greater probability of independence, innovation and variety in the future than starting her own business might do just at present.

Paula can go ahead with her decision knowing that it reflects her values and her sense of purpose in life. She can direct her energy into setting goals and drawing up detailed plans for achieving them with a high degree of motivation and an optimistic, positive belief in her future.

Recap

To overcome indecision you need to:

- Find out what your options are.

- Check them against your values.

- Pick the options that match your values best.

- Anticipate any potential problems and find solutions.

- Go ahead and make an informed, rational choice.

8 The comfort trap

There are many situations and experiences we have encountered so often that we know exactly how to behave and respond to them, and feel completely at home with them. This is the comfort zone – the sum of all the things we have done so often that we feel thoroughly comfortable about doing them again.

We spend most of our time in this comfort zone, doing familiar things. We feel competent and confident there, safe and unchallenged, if sometimes a little bored, unstretched or restricted. The comfort zone can turn into a comfort trap, however.

Why is the comfort zone a problem?

The comfort zone itself is no problem. The problem starts when we have to do, or want to do, something that lies outside it: something new that we haven't done before, or something we've failed at before. Sometimes that makes us feel uncomfortable. We feel safer staying where we are, and that's when the comfort zone becomes the comfort trap.

Finding ourselves faced with the need to do something new or unfamiliar, we can feel out of our depth. The risk we perceive can make us feel anxious, irritable or even angry. We can feel fearful, helpless or guilty, and end up resentful about having to do something that makes us feel so uncomfortable.

Naturally, if these negative feelings are strong enough, they can outweigh any thought of the rewards that the new experience may bring. This leaves us with just the option of doing something familiar, trapped in the comfort zone, afraid to venture out.

When Robert was offered a dream job abroad he was thrilled at first. Then he began worrying about how he would cope in a new environment with a different language where he knew nobody. What if it all went wrong? He nearly made himself sick with anxiety and seriously considered turning the job down.

However much we want the positive results, the negative feelings come to mind first when we think about doing something new. Gradually, we come to automatically associate those negative feelings with the idea of doing something different. The answer? Don't do anything different, and you won't have those negative feelings!

Unfortunately, it's virtually impossible to pursue a purposeful life from the safety of the comfort zone. Most goals require you to do something new or unfamiliar, and you have to risk making mistakes and even failing if you want to acquire new skills and proficiencies.

Naturally positive people use their comfort zone as a launch pad to wider experiences. They work steadily outwards from what feels comfortable, using what they feel familiar with, and competent in, as a firm foundation to build on.

Being realistic, they don't expect things to always be easy and comfortable, and are willing to put up with the temporary discomfort of those negative feelings in order to experience greater feelings of comfort and satisfaction in the long run. The comfort zone is always there for them when they want to rest, relax or recoup their resources, so taking risks becomes less risky.

A valuable consequence of this is that their comfort zone actually increases in size as they become familiar with, and at ease with, a wider and wider range of situations and experiences. By risking discomfort they, paradoxically, achieve even greater comfort.

Overcoming the comfort trap

First, build on your natural courage and intrepidity:

- Understand what is important to you, what you believe is worth taking the risk for.

- Break big goals down into small, manageable steps only just outside your comfort zone.

- Get plenty of rest and relaxation and don't let stress build up.

- Focus on your successes.

- Minimise your failures.

- Look for what's positive and interesting in new opportunities before looking for what might be negative.

- Think about the solutions whenever you anticipate problems.

- Take time to appreciate the rewards and benefits of doing something new, rather than focusing only on the initial feelings of discomfort.

- Know how to learn from your mistakes rather than fearing them.

- Stick with it – doing something regularly will take the sting out of it, even if it seems hard at first

- Don't accept excuses from yourself.

In addition to the above, there are three main keys that will help you to step outside your own comfort zone: you need to confront your fears, build up your confidence, and take reasonable risks.

Confront your fears

The first step in getting outside the comfort zone is to recognise that it's there, and that doing anything new or different can cause negative feelings simply because it *is* new and different, and not because there is anything wrong with doing it.

It's also important to realise that feeling anxious, fearful, helpless, etc. isn't the end of the world; it's just a temporary state. If you can learn to tolerate a degree of discomfort, you will find that it eventually becomes much less threatening altogether. You may even find that positive feelings such as excitement and anticipation have the chance to break through.

Always check back with your values, though. Make sure your reluctance is due only to anticipated discomfort, and not because you are doing something contrary to your beliefs.

Confronting your fears means sorting out your priorities and making choices – is it more important to you to achieve your goal or avoid anxiety? Either choice is valid. Sometimes avoiding anxiety may be a high priority for looking after yourself, at other times pursuing your goals will be more important. There is a difference, though, between making a conscious, reasoned choice and unconsciously reacting out of fear of discomfort.

Build up your confidence

First, let go of your past. Put all your bygone fears, mistakes, embarrassments, anxieties and miscalculations into perspective.

Forgive yourself your past mistakes. They are just an essential part of learning to do anything new, a stepping stone to present and future success. Be tolerant and forgiving of past misunderstandings and errors. Try to look at your past through adult eyes. The chances are, the mistakes you made in the past were due to inexperience. You will probably never make those same mistakes again because you are that much more mature and experienced. As you matured and gained experiences, and through making those very mistakes, you can afford to look back on your younger self with understanding and patience. And look at your past with generosity and kindness. Many people are far harder on themselves than they are on anyone else. Treat yourself with at least the compassion that you have for a friend or colleague.

Next, build up your courage. You can start this right at the beginning of the day by setting your alarm 15 or 20 minutes earlier to give yourself time for the following activities:

- Wake up fully. Get some daylight, fresh air and gentle movement first thing and get off to an optimistic, energetic start (see page 41).

- Smile. Strange as it may sound, a false smile can have exactly the same enlivening effect on the brain and body as a real one. Smile at yourself in the mirror first thing, and set yourself up for the day.

- Try an affirmation – a positive statement that you can repeat to yourself. Used diligently, affirmations effectively replace the negative self-talk that most of us indulge in. Repeat an upbeat and positive affirmation to yourself while you get ready for the day. Possible ones include:

- 'I am looking forward to today with confidence and enthusiasm.'

- 'I'm looking out for all the good things today brings.'

- 'I enjoy the surprises life brings.'

- 'I trust life.'

- 'I enjoy life.'

- Eat a good breakfast to give you energy for the day ahead. To give your spirits a lift, try listening to cheerful music while you eat instead of listening to the news or reading the paper.

- Take a few minutes to decide what you want to achieve during the day – what is important, what you want to do and when you intend to do it.

Having had a good start to the day, set aside a few minutes to end it equally well:

- Before you go to sleep go over the good points of the day, the things you've enjoyed and the things you've learned. Firmly push any anxieties to one side by promising yourself you'll deal with them tomorrow.

- Think of one thing you intend to enjoy tomorrow.

- Lull yourself to sleep with a gentle affirmation, such as:

  - 'I rest deeply and peacefully.'

  - 'I have done well and can now rest fully and completely.'

- 'My days are complete and enjoyable.'

- 'All is as it should be.'

- 'All is well.'

Take reasonable risks

Stepping out of your comfort zone means taking some well-calculated risks. You risk feeling uncomfortable, making mistakes, being out of your depth and doing things that are unfamiliar. You can minimise the stress of risk-taking by continuing to move outwards, expanding your comfort zone, without over-burdening your ability to cope.

Before taking any sort of risk, decide what the worst possible thing that could result from it would be, and plan what you would do if that happened. How would you recover? When mistakes and miscalculations occur, know how to cope with them. The worst way is to ignore the problem, run away from it, or pretend that nothing is wrong. The best way is to acknowledge the mistake and propose a way of rectifying it. Handling mistakes effectively is usually a matter of experience – the more you make the better you get at it.

Your comfort zone is there for you to renew your energies. Balance excitement with routine, challenge with familiarity, and stimulation with rest and ease. But make sure you take action instead of waiting to be rescued. You'll be disappointed, and suffer uncomfortable feelings of resentment and frustration when the rescue doesn't happen. Go out and live instead. Go after what you want rather than waiting for it to drop into your comfort zone.

Before taking a risk, plan it thoroughly and break things down into small steps rather than trying to achieve everything at once.

Surprisingly, it's not the big steps that are the most important, it's just the willingness to do *something* that moves you outside your comfort zone. If you are hesitating about taking some course of action, ask yourself what is the minimum you would be willing to do? Some examples might be:

TASK OUTSIDE MY COMFORT ZONE	MINIMUM I WOULD BE WILLING TO DO
Speaking in public	Read a short, prepared introduction for a guest speaker.
Writing a novel	Sit and write for 20 minutes a day, every day.
Apply for a new job	Talk to a couple of professional colleagues about what's happening in the industry.

If a step outside your comfort zone seems impossible or too uncomfortable to contemplate, keep breaking it down into gentler and gentler stages until you reach something you feel happy with. When you've tackled that successfully, ask yourself what's the next minimum you'd be prepared to do.

Close your eyes and recall a time when you tried something new or unfamiliar that worked out well. Enjoy reliving the experience in your imagination. Enjoy recreating the invigorating feelings you had then, and look forward to experiencing them again in the future.

Recap

Overcome your dependence on the comfort zone by:

- Building on your natural courage and intrepidity.

- Confronting your fears and putting them into perspective.

- Building up your confidence:

  - be tolerant of your mistakes and failures

  - put yourself in a courageous frame of mind each morning

  - put yourself in a positive frame of mind each evening.

- Taking reasonable risks:

  - learn how to take the stress out of risk-taking.

9 Hurry sickness

Hurry sickness, crisis addiction, urgency syndrome – whatever you call it – means you end up dashing wildly from one appointment to another without time for lunch, working late to meet last-minute deadlines, and putting friends and family on hold while you schedule in yet another meeting.

The 'symptoms' of hurry sickness can include:

- reluctance to stop and think

- restlessness and sudden boredom

- impatience with details

- disinclination to plan effectively and thoroughly

- crises that crop up with more than normal frequency

- unease at the thought of being 'idle'

- panic at the thought of being alone with nothing to do

- no time to spare for anything less than very urgent tasks

- inability to distinguish between what is urgent and what is important

- constantly doing two or three things at once

- inability to give full, focused attention to anything for long

- reluctance to 'waste time' looking after yourself

- lack of interest in anything outside immediate concerns and problems

- the temptation to cram 'just one more thing' into the schedule

- frequently running late for appointments

- seeing yourself as a 'fire-fighter' or 'troubleshooter'.

Why do people suffer from hurry sickness?

Although it sounds very different from the comfort trap, hurry sickness serves a very similar purpose: security. It prevents the sufferer from ever having to examine their life and take the risk of going after what they truly want. If you can cram your life with crises, you will never have time, even if you briefly have the inclination, to think about whether your life is purposeful or happy. You're busy, and that's all the matters.

Ellen was on the go from morning to night dealing with housework, the garden, her husband and two small children. Although she often said that she wished she could go back to her old job in education, it was clear to everybody that there was no time for it – Ellen barely had a spare moment in her day. Her husband and other members of the family often offered to help but Ellen always turned them down, saying it was quicker and easier to do it herself.

Eventually, the children started school and Ellen was finally free to return to her career. Unfortunately, she had just contracted builders for a new conservatory and kitchen extension and the garden would need replanning, she had become involved with two local committees, her husband needed her encouragement to get the promotion he deserved and, of course, the children still needed her support.

Being busy makes all of us feel important and useful. We're needed, we don't know how they'd manage without us, and that's very validating. However, rather than just being busy, we could be even more useful if we put that effort into planning and doing things that fit our values, purpose and roles in life. Finding your life purpose may not be urgent, but it is important.

Why is hurry sickness a problem?

If you always do what's urgent, you will never get around to doing what's important. Responding to instant crises takes the centre of control out of your hands and leaves the direction your life takes entirely up to random outside forces. Without that feeling of control, not only is life ultimately aimless, but stress is also a real problem.

Natural positive thinkers have purposeful, complete lives, yet rarely seem harassed or rushed. They take more risks than average, and often accomplish a great deal, yet seldom appear frazzled by crises. They are nearly always able to distinguish clearly between what is urgent and what is important and they can prioritise accordingly. They can pace themselves without feeling the need to rush, and they are quite prepared to delegate and even say no when necessary.

Slow down

For a change of pace:

- Find out what is important to you and learn to make it a high priority.

- Make a plan and set goals and targets for yourself.

- Understand what else motivates you, besides urgency.

- Aim for a healthy, balanced lifestyle that includes rest and recreation.

- Learn how to replace bad habits with positive ones.

- Be honest with yourself.

When you're in the grip of hurry sickness it's very difficult to understand that it is almost entirely self-generated, especially as crises and urgencies crop up from time to time in everybody's life.

Try letting go of some of the urgency and see what happens, though. Tackle it step by step, starting with something easy – maybe stopping for a 20-minute lunch break every day – and working your way up from there. Remember to reward yourself when you achieve a target – stopping for a lunch break five days out of five, for example.

After a long talk with her husband, Ellen discovered that her feelings about going back to work were much more complicated than she'd imagined. While in theory it was what she wanted, in fact she was anxious about being back in a competitive, demanding environment and feared she might not be up to it. She was also surprised to realise that she actually very much enjoyed tending to the house and garden and using her creative side to enhance them.

Ellen decided to slow down, take more time for herself and find out what she really wanted before making any decisions. She discovered she had many more options than either staying at home or going back to work and found she was quite excited about her future possibilities.

To help yourself slow down it's important to establish your priorities (see page 20). Your highest priorities are those things that reflect your values and are part of the roles you play. Think seriously about all the urgent crises that crop up that have nothing to do with either. How do they come about? Why are they your responsibility? At the very least, take 5 minutes every morning to *write down* a list of your top priorities (real priorities – things that are important, not just urgent) for the day, and a schedule into which they can be slotted. Allow more time than you think you need for them. Allocate half as much time again to any undertaking – from finishing a report, to getting to the station, to making friends with a new neighbour.

Think through jobs and courses of action before you start. Ensure that you have the time and all the resources you need, rather than having to crisis-manage running out of either in the middle. During the day focus on one task at a time. Relax and breathe slowly and deeply when you feel the urge to abandon it for something else. Do it well, do it thoroughly, and finish it before moving on to something else. Resist the urge to push plans and relationships. Watch and listen for feedback before proceeding to the next stage. In particular, listen to other people when they talk, and let conversations develop at their own pace.

Look after yourself (see page 42) and make time to eat, sleep and take exercise. Schedule in the bare minimum and work up – even a little bit is always better than nothing. One of the hardest things to do is to take time to relax. Start with 5 minutes a day, scheduled for the same time every day – don't wait until you have a spare moment, or until you feel like it. When it's time to relax just close your eyes and do nothing for 5 minutes precisely. Reward yourself when you achieve it seven days out of seven.

Cutting something out is even harder than finding time to relax, but it is definitely well on the way to living without hurry sickness. Start easing out all the things that don't relate to your life-purpose and values. Set yourself a clear target – aim to cut one meeting a week out of your schedule, for example, or hand over your club treasurer's position to someone else by the end of the year. Reward yourself when you achieve a target, and then move on to the next one.

Recap

If you would like to help yourself to overcome hurry sickness:

• Shift your focus from what's urgent to what's important.

• Slow down and take time to concentrate on what you're doing:

  • establish your priorities

  • think and plan ahead rather than waiting for crises to dictate what you should be doing

  • remember that time spent looking after yourself is never wasted

  • cut out what isn't important.

10 Demand thinking

Sometimes, particularly when things are most important to us, we become rather tense and inflexible about getting what we want – we *demand* that a thing should be so rather than *preferring* that it should be:

- We **must** get what we want; it would be awful if we didn't.

- We **must** not have to go through this; it would mean the end of the world.

- It **must** happen; we can't bear it otherwise.

- We **have** to have that; it's unthinkable otherwise.

When Kate applied for a promotion and didn't get it, she was disappointed but was able to swallow her chagrin and ask for feedback about why she had failed. As a result, she was able to improve her performance and her next application was successful. When Beth didn't get promoted she was furious. She felt betrayed, mortified and belittled and resigned shortly afterwards because of the shabby way she believed she'd been treated.

Kate was a positive, realistic thinker who ultimately achieved her aim. Beth, on the other hand, robbed herself of any subsequent opportunity for promotion because of her demand thinking. She *had* to achieve her goal and it was *unbearable* when she didn't.

When we set up expectations and make demands on ourselves, other people and life in general it almost guarantees disappointment. Going after the things we want becomes a risky business fraught with frustration, tension and distress, rather than the pleasurable, satisfying, light-hearted activity that it should be.

In particular, we often unconsciously demand that:

* Effort *must* be rewarded (and it's *awful* when it's not).

* We *must* be considered and respected (and it's *dreadful* when we're not).

* Love, kindness, goodwill, etc. *must* be returned (and it's *terrible* when they aren't).

* Things *must not* be too difficult (and it's *intolerable* when they are).

* We *must not* suffer discomfort (and it's *unbearable* if we have to).

Why are we so demanding?

When we were babies, tiny and nearly helpless, our needs were very straightforward and getting them met was, literally, a matter of life and death. As babies we *must* have food and it really is terrible if we don't; we *must* have warmth, and we *will* die if we don't; we *must* have attention and it really *will* be the end of the world if we don't get it.

Now that we're adults, however, we can afford to be a little more flexible in our outlook. Being denied or rejected by our parents would have been fatal; being denied or rejected by our employer, spouse, colleague or friend is much less disastrous.

Why is demand thinking a problem?

The intensity of the demand is matched by the intensity of the disappointment and discomfort we anticipate if we don't get what we want. This, naturally, makes us rather driven and anxious about the outcome. We retreat back into our comfort zone, afraid to risk such damaging consequences even when the rewards of doing so are high.

The result is often a self-fulfilling prophecy. We put so much emotional investment into the result – we want it so badly and are so afraid of failing – that we don't see the opportunities and take the calculated risks necessary to achieve it. We consequently often end up more uncomfortable, less satisfied and more anxious than if we had been less intensely demanding in the first place.

People who are naturally positive thinkers take things much more lightly. They would like things to happen, they would prefer things to happen, they take vigorous action to ensure that what they want has an excellent chance of happening. But it wouldn't be an absolute, devastating catastrophe if it didn't. They don't have the same intense emotional attachment to a specific, inflexible outcome. Paradoxically, they are much more likely to get what they desire.

Cultivate preferences

To overcome demand thinking you can cultivate preferences in the place of demands. Preferences are much more positive than demands. They are based on expectation, anticipation and enjoyment, whereas demands are based on fear, dread and anxiety.

Preferences can be pursued with as much passion as demands. With less negative emotional attachment to the outcome, however, failure is much less threatening.

This means that you can risk being more flexible. You can set about getting preferences met much more easily, and with a much more open-minded and positive attitude, than you can with demands. You can be more creative and inventive about both the method and the results – less driven, blinkered and inflexible. You need to take conscious action to turn your demands into preferences.

Recognise demand thinking

You need to recognise when you are being driven by a demand before you can turn it into a preference. There are usually clear signals that you are becoming intense and anxious about a want or desire:

- Physical tension. Your nervous system becomes stimulated and you can't stay calm and relaxed about what you want. Your stomach tightens; you become tense just thinking about it.

- Negative emotions. Rather than pleasure at the thought of what you want, you feel negative emotions such as anxiety, frustration, resentment, anger or fear at the thought of not achieving it or of losing it.

- 'Catastrophising'. You imagine feeling terrible, or what terrible things will happen, if you don't get what you want.

- Obsession. Your thoughts and feelings keep returning to the subject. You find it hard to let things take their course, or to get on with other tasks.

When you notice these warning signs, look for underlying demand. Ask yourself what you feel *must* or *must not* happen, and what you fear the consequences to be.

Preference words

The most effective way of changing demands into preferences is to consciously and persistently change the actual words we use when talking about what we want, need and expect.

Whether talking to other people or thinking about things to yourself, substitute 'preference' words for 'demand' words. Here are some examples:

DEMAND WORD	PREFERENCE WORD
must	prefer
ought	like
should	can
have to	may
got to	hope

By using different words rigorously and consistently, you can consciously build up a more positive way of thinking, feeling and behaving.

Positive statements

When you catch yourself being driven by a demand or catastrophising about an outcome, try replacing negative statements with positive ones. For example:

DEMAND	PREFERENCE
My employer *must* treat me fairly, and if he doesn't that means he's a terrible person and I am a worthless one.	I would *prefer* my employer to treat me well but if he doesn't I can assertively take steps to remedy the situation.
You *must* like me, and if you don't you're cruel, unfair and damaging.	I'd *prefer* you to like me, but if you don't I'll just spend more time with people who do.
My efforts *must* be rewarded amply, and if they aren't it's a great tragedy.	I'd *like* my efforts to be rewarded, but if they aren't, that's life. I've enjoyed myself anyway.

Demand sabotage

Try also to become aware of the way that demands can sabotage your goals and purpose.

Ian was very anxious about meeting his new girlfriend's parents for lunch at their house. He felt it was terribly important he made a good impression and that it would be a catastrophe if he got it wrong. He was so tense and nervous that he stammered and stuttered throughout the meal, upset a glass of wine and broke a plate when he rushed to help clear the table.

Fortunately, Ian got a second chance. The next time he met his girl-friend's parents he knew things couldn't be any worse than they were before so he felt he had nothing to lose. While he would have preferred that they liked him, it didn't matter so much to him if they didn't. He took time to calm down and think about what he wanted to happen, how he wanted to behave this time, and what he would do if he felt himself becoming stressed. Everything went much better. Ian relaxed and chatted without difficulty and found he shared an interest in military aircraft with his girlfriend's father. After that, everything was easy.

Visualisation

It's not always easy to recognise demands for what they are and to remember to turn them into preferences but this visualisation exercise can help.

Follow the relaxation exercises on page 43 to help relax the physical tension associated with demands. While you are relaxed, imagine yourself behaving positively and effectively. Visualise enjoying putting your preferences into effect, rather than being driven by demands.

Recall a time when you found yourself reacting negatively because of a demand. Now see yourself responding calmly and rationally instead; what do you say, what do you do, how do you feel?

Imagine yourself being more much relaxed about outcomes in the future. Imagine not getting what you want. Rather than catastrophising and telling yourself that it's awful, terrible, unbearable, see yourself responding with a shrug as you move on to the next thing. What do you say to yourself, what do you do, how do you feel?

Recap

If you need to overcome demand thinking:

- Learn to recognise the 'symptoms' of a demand.

- Replace demands with preferences:

  - replace demanding words with more relaxing ones

  - replace negative, demanding statements with more positive ones

  - replace catastrophic outcomes with more realistic ones.

- Recognise how demands actually sabotage your intentions.

11 Making comparisons

One thing that is almost certain to sabotage a positive approach to life is making comparisons, yet we do it all the time. We find ourselves comparing ourselves to others or to an ideal, and our present lives to a fantasy idea or a golden past.

While there is value in encouraging the best from ourselves, and in living up to our own standards, there is little to be gained from trying to see how well or badly we do in comparison to other people. Hearing that someone has achieved promotion in a job that holds no interest for us, mastered a skill that has no appeal for us, or attained a position at odds with our values, shouldn't cause us to negatively question our own performance. But sometimes it does, especially when our self-esteem is at a low ebb.

Why do we compare ourselves to others?

We have a natural curiosity, and a tendency to see how we measure up to others. When we are young, this helps us to develop – to find our place in the community, and to appreciate the stages we will ourselves achieve during growing up.

This natural tendency to find out where we fit in can easily develop into competition, however, and is sometimes encouraged from an early age. As we get older we're ranked against each other in exams and sports, and often actively encouraged to become competitive. While not intrinsically bad, comparisons like these can take on a negative edge when there are rewards and punishments for success or failure. Our own performance becomes of less value than our performance compared to others.

It's not surprising that, as adults, we find ourselves comparing our attainments, our lifestyle, even our values and commitments to those of others. It's also of little surprise that we feel anxious if we perceive a failure to measure up to others.

Why are comparisons a problem?

Competition and comparison focus our attention on what others are doing and how they are performing, rather than focusing it on what we want to do. They distract us from our purpose in life and lead to unnecessary, unhelpful questions about what we *should* be doing (in comparison to everyone else) or what we *ought* to be doing (in comparison to everyone else). We might also start worrying about what other people think of our values and purpose in life. Will they approve of them and think them worthwhile?

Nina greatly enjoyed writing short stories for women's magazines. She was successful and put thought and effort into making each story just that little bit different and unusual. She understood her market and delighted in spinning yarns that she knew would engage and amuse her readers. Unfortunately, her sister-in-law tended to look down on what she called chick-lit and frequently berated Nina for, as she saw it, wasting her talent. Why didn't Nina emulate the literary heavyweights such as X or Y? Why didn't Nina write a proper novel or at least some serious stories instead of the disposable froth that she did?

Eventually Nina began to doubt herself and feel guilty – perhaps she *was* wasting her talent; perhaps she should try something more demanding. After all, wasn't what she was doing rather frivolous and self-indulgent? It certainly wasn't very meaningful. She started, but didn't finish, several stories on more serious themes, became hesitant about what she was writing and even began to develop writers' block.

Happily, she met someone at a conference who told her how much she enjoyed Nina's stories and looked out for them because they had given her a much-needed means of escape when she was going through a traumatic divorce. This gave Nina the perspective she needed and she was able to return to doing what she loved with a lighter heart.

Constant comparison can make us question our intentions, undermine our sense of purpose and motivations, and cause negative states such as jealousy, anxiety, egotism, shame, hopelessness, uncertainty, anger and defeat. At its extreme, persistent comparison with others can lead to conformity, passivity, lack of identity, perceived inferiority, insecurity, possessiveness and hostile competitiveness.

Naturally positive people have a strong tendency to measure themselves only against their own standards and not against other people. They are firmly grounded in themselves and, while they admire and respect the achievement of others, they rarely feel that they have to compete with them.

Interestingly, some of the happiest, healthiest, most positive people have been found to be those who could be called natural eccentrics. Although they may take things to extremes, they have a very strong sense of purpose based exclusively on their own values, and pay very little attention, if any, to what anyone else thinks of them. This makes them very secure in themselves and encourages an optimistic, positive approach to life.

Cultivate individuality and independence

In order to stop making comparisons, understand what your own individual values, roles and purpose in life are and set your goals and plan your action accordingly. Focus on your successes and appreciate that they are due to your own individual talent and hard work. Understand what motivates you, and what you find rewarding.

Become consciously aware of when, where and how you compare yourself with others, or find yourself competing with them. Develop your own ideas, thoughts, opinions and activities, and recognise and accept that you have a right to your individual values, just as others have a right to theirs.

Become aware of making comparisons

When you find yourself making comparisons, stop. Focus instead on the positive things about yourself and your life. Notice when you compare yourself to anyone else, or to some unrealisable ideal. Write it down – this record will help you to pick up any recurring themes or underlying patterns.

Victoria is an illustrator who recently took the daunting step of moving to the country and going freelance to improve her quality of life, but she sometimes wonders if she's done the right thing. She noted down any comparisons she made during the week:

Monday Visit H. Admire new flat and find myself wishing I lived in the city instead of the country. Uncertain that I've made the right move.

Tuesday Read magazine. Admire thin models. Feel insecure and unattractive. Wonder if I should go on a diet.

Wednesday D promoted. Remember that it could have been me if I'd stayed with J&J and feel jealous.

Thursday See romantic film. Wonder why I don't have that sort of relationship and feel anxious and rejected.

Friday Meet R. Feel slightly superior because baby means she can't work and is financially dependent on T.

Next, she wrote a rebuttal to the comparison, focusing on positive things and, where possible, recalling her values:

Monday Visit H. Admire new flat and find myself wishing I lived in the city instead of the country. Uncertain that I've made the right move.

Recall original reasons for move: more space, better air, good for walks, more peaceful. In keeping with my value of a simple, healthy life (rather than a glamorous one!).

Tuesday Read magazine. Admire thin models. Feel insecure and unattractive. Wonder if I should go on a diet.

I already eat a good nourishing diet. Feel and look healthy and energetic because of it.

Wednesday D promoted. Remember that it could have been me if I'd stayed with J&J and feel jealous.

I left J&J to go freelance in line with my values of independence and creativity (I didn't want to be promoted into management).

Thursday See romantic film. Wonder why I don't have that sort of relationship and feel anxious and rejected.

It's fiction! Nobody has a relationship like that. Remember values of independence and equality.

Friday Meet R. Feel slightly superior because baby means she can't work and is financially dependent on T.

Independence is one of my values, not R's. Her values are entirely different and just as good. She is doing what she wants to do. I am doing what I want to do.

Continuing this exercise over a period of time should help you bring your attention back to yourself and your concerns rather than focusing negatively on comparisons with other people.

Get to know yourself better

Reflecting on your values is an excellent way to get to know yourself better. You can also put yourself in contact with yourself and remind yourself who you are and how you might have changed by completing the following statements. Take time to think about them and actually write down the answers so you can look back over them later:

The five words that describe me best are . . .

The five things I most enjoy doing are . . .

I currently feel strongly about . . .

I have been most affected recently by . . .

When I was little I wanted to be . . .

Today I want to be . . .

My childhood hero/ine is . . .

I am at my best . . .

I am happy when . . .

I am proudest of . . .

I would give up everything for . . .

I wouldn't give up . . . for anything

I would like . . . to be recognised and appreciated

If I could do what I wanted right now, I would . . .

If I could do what I wanted next week, I would . . .

If I could do what I wanted for the rest of my life, I would . . .

The five things I think are most important are . . .

. . . makes me feel hopeful.

. . . makes me laugh.

I always thought I would grow up to . . .

I am most glad that I . . .

There are no right or wrong answers. The statements are simply there to focus your attention on what you think, feel and believe.

Recognise your rights

It helps to remember that everybody – yourself included – has certain basic rights. These can be useful if you feel a bit insecure or uncertain of your individuality. Recalling your rights can help you to feel clear about the value of having your own ideas and beliefs; here's a list:

1. I have the right to make my own decisions.

2. I have the right to decide what I want.

3. I have the right to decide what I need.

4. I have the right to decide what I like or don't like.

5. I have the right to make my own mistakes.

6. I have the right to have self-respect.

7. I have the right to express my own feelings.

8. I have the right to express my own opinions.

9. I have the right to express my own values.

10. I have the right to say yes or no as I decide appropriate.

11. I have the right to change my mind.

(And so does every other human being on this planet.)

Repeat your rights to yourself frequently. They allow you to appreciate the values and opinions of others while focusing your attention firmly on your own.

Recap

If you would like to help yourself to overcome making comparisons:

- Become aware of when and where you tend to compare yourself or compete with others:
  - notice how you compare yourself
  - counter the comparisons with positive statements.
- Get to know and appreciate your own ideas and opinions better.
- Understand your rights.

Conclusion
Become a positive thinker

Becoming a positive thinker isn't difficult but it does require deliberate effort. Slipping into the habit of negative thinking may happen over a period of years and it can take conscious determination to replace negative habits with more rewarding positive ones.

Beat the negative cycle

One of the problems is that negativity becomes a self-fulfilling prophecy. Negative beliefs lead to negative expectations which lead to negative behaviour which produces a negative result which reinforces the original negative belief and increases negative expectations which leads to further negative behaviour which . . . well, you see what I mean:

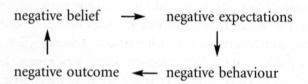

Happily, positive habits behave in just the same manner of self-perpetuation. Positive beliefs build up positive expectations, which lead you to behave in a positive way, which produces a positive outcome, which reinforces your positive beliefs, and so on.

Because it's a cycle, it doesn't matter if you start with a positive belief, expectation or behaviour, when you try to change from a negative cycle to a positive one. You can start anywhere, wherever is easiest. Indeed, the change from a negative to a positive cycle sometimes happens accidentally when someone experiences an unexpected positive outcome – a 'stroke of luck' – that changes their beliefs and expectations. You don't have to wait for luck, though; you can take active steps to change your life for the better and become a positive thinker any time.

All of us were born with a capacity for positive thinking that served us well during early childhood. We acquired the habit of negative thinking as we grew up and experienced negative attitudes and discouragement from the world around us. Just as we learned to be pessimistic, so we can learn to regain our positivity and optimism by doing what natural positive thinkers do.

James felt he had no luck in relationships. He was good-looking and had no trouble asking girls out, but after a few dates things just seemed to fizzle out. He kept wondering why he was so unlucky with the sort of girls he was meeting. When James looked more deeply into his problem, however, he found he was perpetuating a negative cycle. It had started when a girl he very much admired had dumped him because, she said, she found him boring company. This dented his self-confidence and, although he'd never had any problems with friends in the past, it started him thinking that 'girls want something more'. The negative cycle was begun: James believed he was a dull companion, which led to the expectation that any girl would be bored by him and so he tried to compensate, alternating between being over-hesitant and over-effusive. This led to uncomfortable dates that girls, understandably, didn't want to repeat, reinforcing James's belief that he was boring company, and so the cycle continued.

James needed to break it somewhere. He could consciously change his beliefs, maybe repeating affirmations that he was an interesting and worthwhile person or remembering that other friends enjoyed his company. He could change his expectations and look for evidence that his date was enjoying being with him. He could monitor and change his behaviour so that he was neither hesitant nor effusive but just acting the way he did with other people. He could also, of course, just wait until he found a girl who didn't object to his behaviour and wanted to see him again – a positive outcome regardless of a negative cycle, that he'd been unconsciously hoping would simply happen.

James decided to consciously change his behaviour and see what developed. Although still a little anxious, he remained optimistic and positive and soon saw the sort of changes that rebuilt his self-belief. His relaxed, unforced behaviour – the way he usually was with friends – led to an enjoyable date for both parties. This made James believe that he was a pleasant, not boring, companion, and created an expectation that any girl would be happy in his company. This confident approach reinforced his relaxed behaviour in a girl's company, and so James found that he had successfully initiated a positive cycle which rapidly became self-perpetuating.

Ready to go!

Change your negative habits: start now. Begin anywhere you like and see how the benefits begin to mount up as you develop positive, self-sustaining cycles. Don't worry about getting it all right all the time, just begin with the easiest things you can change and go on from there. You are probably already much closer to living a positive life than you imagine. Ask yourself:

• What are the existing positive things in your life?

• What do you already know, believe or have already done, that will help you achieve a positive life?

• Which of your existing achievements will help you?

• What challenges have you already met and overcome?

Think about how you are going to build a positive life tailored specifically to your own unique needs. Build on what you already know:

• Which strategies have worked best in the past?

• Which ones bring you closer to what you want?

• Which ones move you away from what you want?

• What are three positive actions you could do from today that would take you closer to what you want?

And remember...

To help you take your own positive steps, don't forget these three simple principles:

• *Focus on the positive.* Look out for positive things – search out the positive aspects of situations and events. Spend time with positive people; encourage positive attitudes; look for opportunities to enjoy yourself and focus on pleasant things. Minimise the time you spend dwelling on negative things, and avoid as much as possible people and things that lower your energy and make you feel down.

- *Speak positively to yourself.* Change the voice in your head from one that criticises and complains into one that supports and encourages you. Concentrate on making positive statements to yourself about yourself, your behaviour and the world in general.

- *Act positively.* You don't have to wait. Pretend you already *are* a positive person – have a purpose in life, look for solutions, be supportive and encouraging to yourself and others. Hold your head up, put your shoulders back and smile. Look positive and you will feel positive. Give yourself positive feedback at every opportunity.

You can achieve an interesting, rewarding, fulfilling life for yourself. Everything is possible. Good luck!

Quick reference
Common complaints

This section looks at some common worries and difficulties, such as feeling anxious, indecisive, or not being able to sleep. You'll find three positive-thinking answers for each complaint, so you can choose the most relevant one depending on whether you have 5 minutes, 20 minutes to an hour, or you want a long-term plan.

I feel really angry

5 minute cure: Punch a pillow.
20 minute–1 hour cure: Go for a run.
Long-term plan: Write a list of all the things you feel angry about and then think calmly about what you'd rather have happen in each case. Is there anything you could do, now you're feeling calm, to improve the situation?

I feel anxious and afraid

5 minute cure: Take a couple of deep breaths; hold your head up and pull your shoulders back. Smile. Tell yourself, 'This is a challenge I'm ready for', 'I am strong, courageous and confident', or 'I am calm, alert and ready'.
20 minute–1 hour cure: Build a 'safe place' in your imagination

that you can use when you feel anxious and stressed. Breathe deeply and close your eyes. Relax each group of muscles in your body in turn, starting at your feet and working upwards. When you feel physically relaxed, imagine a tranquil, peaceful place – maybe a garden or a tropical beach. Imagine it in detail and immerse yourself in the sights, sounds, smells, taste and feeling of the place. When you feel ready, come back to the everyday world. Whenever you need time out, return to your tranquil spot.

Long-term plan: Tackle the source of your anxiety. Write a list of all the things you feel anxious about and think calmly about what you'd rather have happen in each case. Take all the practical steps you can to improve the situation.

I need more confidence

5 minute cure: When was the last time your confidence got a boost? Close your eyes and think back to that event in detail – pretend that you're there again.

20 minute–1 hour cure: At the end of each day, think back over what you've done well and note it down in a diary. Find at least one thing a day. When you need a confidence boost, look back over it.

Long-term plan: Set yourself a series of mini-challenges that lead you towards a worthwhile goal. Success breeds confidence.

I feel directionless

5 minute cure: Note down some key words about how you would like your life to be and put them where you'll see them frequently.

20 minute–1 hour cure: Make a life-map. Using a big sheet of card, cut and stick pictures from magazines that represent the things you would like to have in your life. Put it where you will see it.

Long-term plan: Think of three things you would like to achieve. Devise a goal for each one, broken down into the steps you need to take to achieve it.

I feel down

5 minute cure: Listen to cheerful, upbeat music.

20 minute–1 hour cure: Read a book, watch a television programme or DVD, or see a film that you can rely on to be amusing.

Long-term plan: Devise a plan for getting more joy into your life on a regular basis. Include positive experiences at regular intervals: list ten things that give you pleasure and decide which you are going to include every day; which once a week; which once or twice a month; and which a couple of times a year.

I need more energy

5 minute cure: Stand in front of an open window. Breathe in and stretch.

20 minute–1 hour cure: Find some upbeat, high-energy music and dance.

Long-term plan: Look at your lifestyle – diet, exercise, sleep, etc. Make three changes that you know will improve your health.

I feel envious

5 minute cure: Change your internal voice. Instead of saying, 'It's not fair', 'They don't deserve that', 'Why do they have all the luck', try saying, 'That's something I'd like to have', 'I can achieve that too', 'That's worth the effort it must have taken'.

20 minute–1 hour cure: Remind yourself what's good about your own life. Write down what you are happy about, what you are proud of, what you enjoy and who supports and appreciates you.

Long-term plan: Use your envy to alert you to what you want in life. Set goals to attain it and plan the achievable steps you will take to reach it.

I feel that I'm a failure

5 minute cure: Act like a success – head up, shoulders back, big smile.

20 minute–1 hour cure: Change the voice in your head that tells you you're a failure. Write down the negative words and phrases and replace them with positive ones.

Long-term plan: List the obstacles preventing you from being successful. What will you do to overcome them? Do you need support or resources? How will you make sure you get them?

I feel indecisive

5 minute cure: Toss a coin – heads for one option, tails for the other. How do you feel about the result?

20 minute–1 hour cure: List three options (or more if you have them, but certainly no fewer) and beside each one write the pros and cons. Which looks like the best option?

Long-term plan: Make a full evaluation of your options based on how well each one reflects your values. See page 94 for a good method.

I feel irritable

5 minute cure: Close your eyes and take a deep breath. Imagine yourself surrounded by a sphere of blue light. Smile – even if you don't feel like it at first, the smile will become easier as you do it.

20 minute–1 hour cure: Take a warm, scented bath, with candle-light if possible. As you soak, imagine the water dissolving all your irritation. Think of it swirling away down the plughole with the water as you empty the bath.

Long-term plan: If you regularly feel irritated, check your diet. Low blood sugar, stimulants or dehydration can all make you snappy. Cut back on sugar and caffeine in particular, and also saturated fat, salt and alcohol. Stock up on fruit, vegetables and whole grains, and drink more water and herbal teas.

I need a lift

5 minute cure: Look in the mirror and give yourself a big, cheesy grin. Your body can't tell the difference between a false smile and a real one so smile often and you will actually feel happier.

20 minute–1 hour cure: Write about a happy memory you have. Visualise it in the brightest colours and describe it in the most imaginative and evocative words. Don't forget sound, smell and feelings as well as sight in your description.

Long-term plan: Start a scrapbook for inspiration. Include pictures of things you love, people who are close to you, events you enjoy, inspiring quotations and things that make you laugh. Work on it regularly and look through it often.

I lack motivation

5 minute cure: Promise yourself a specific reward when you've finished.

20 minute–1 hour cure: Visualise the outcome you want and write down all the benefits and rewards you will get when you succeed.

Long-term plan: Build up a bank of people who can encourage you, listen to you and give you practical help or information. Make time at least once a month to talk through plans, share your dreams, celebrate your successes, and bemoan your failures with them. Remember to return the favour!

I feel overwhelmed

5 minute cure: Stop and be in the moment. Where are you? What can you see, hear, smell? How do you feel, physically?

20 minute–1 hour cure: What are the 'shoulds', 'musts' and 'oughts' that are running your life? Write them down and change those words into 'prefer' and 'like'.

Long-term plan: Identify three things that drain your energy and that you would prefer to eliminate from your life. Devise a plan for getting rid of them.

I keep putting things off

5 minute cure: Whatever it is you're putting off, do it for just 5 minutes and see how you feel about it at the end of that time.

20 minute–1 hour cure: What is the worst that can happen if you do it? Write down all the possibilities and, next to them, what you will do if they happen, how you will cope.

Long-term plan: Decide what your goal is and write down all the steps involved. Break it down until each step seems like something possible. What's the smallest step you could start with? What are the three steps you could take today?

I need to relax

5 minute cure: Breathe in slowly for a count of four, hold for four and breathe out for a count of five. Repeat five times.

20 minute–1 hour cure: Sit or lie quietly with your eyes closed.

Starting at your feet, work your way through each group of muscles tensing them for 5 seconds then letting go. Finish by taking a deep breath and letting it go.

Long-term plan: Devise a plan for getting more relaxation into your life on a regular basis. Buy a relaxation CD and use it regularly – preferably every day. Try a T'ai Chi or yoga session once a week. Have an aromatherapy massage once a month. Take a relaxing break to pamper yourself once or twice a year.

I feel self-conscious

5 minute cure: Remember SOFT: Smile; use Open body language – head up, shoulders back, open gestures; Face Forward and lean slightly towards people to show interest; use Touch to establish contact – a handshake, light shoulder or arm touch.

20 minute–1 hour cure: Before going into the situation, visualise how you want things to go. See yourself taking an interest in others and putting them at their ease.

Long-term plan: Learn how to perform confidently in public – join a drama or other performance group, or learn public speaking.

I can't sleep

5 minute cure: Try a cup of chamomile tea to soothe you, ear-plugs to cut out noise, and an eye-mask to cut out light.

20 minute–1 hour cure: Write out your thoughts on paper, especially any persistent worries. Put them aside to deal with in the morning.

Long-term plan: Make sure you get enough daylight, fresh air and exercise during the day and establish a relaxing routine for about an hour before you go to bed – a warm bath, comfortable clothes, hot drink, soothing music, etc. – so that your body and mind can prepare. Keep your bedroom just for sleeping, no television or computer or anything else that might prove too stimulating.

I can't stick at things

5 minute cure: Write yourself a contract – 'I, X, will do xyz . . .' – and sign and date it. Put it where you'll see it.

20 minute–1 hour cure: Identify three things you've succeeded at. For each one write down three things it's taught you.

Long-term plan: Identify your values. Ask yourself how you express your values in your daily life and how the thing you want to stick at fits in with that.

I feel really stressed

5 minute cure: Breathe in to the count of five. Hold your breath and shrug your shoulders up towards your ears. Breathe out to a count of five. Repeat.

20 minute–1 hour cure: Go for a brisk walk.

Long-term plan: Find time every day – preferably at the same time every day – to sit still in silence and quieten your mind.

I feel tired in the morning

5 minute cure: Open a window, take a deep breath in and stretch.

20 minute–1 hour cure: Take a short walk in the fresh air.

Long-term plan: Review your sleeping arrangements. Get enough gentle exercise during the day and set up a relaxing bedtime routine. Get enough sleep by going to bed early rather than waking late. Avoid using your bedroom as an office if at all possible so that you associate it with rest and relaxation rather than work and worry.

I've got too much to do

5 minute cure: List your tasks. Pick one that takes 5 minutes to do. Do it. Cross it off the list.

20 minute–1 hour cure: List your tasks. Go through them deciding on the three 'D's: Do, Delegate or Dump.

Long-term plan: Establish your priorities. What three things do you want to achieve in the coming year? What three things do you want to achieve in the next 3 months? What three things do you want to achieve tomorrow? Focus on these and get everything else done and out of the way as quickly and efficiently as possible if you can't delegate or dump it.

Things haven't worked out as I'd hoped

5 minute cure: Think about what you did well and what you would do differently another time.

20 minute–1 hour cure: Do a full PIN assessment: What is Positive about what's happened? What is Interesting? What is Negative? Write down at least three solutions or things you will do differently for each negative point.

Long-term plan: Establish what you want to do differently in the future. List what changes to your beliefs, expectations and behaviour will have to happen to make it possible. Plan how you are going to accomplish those changes in small, achievable steps.

Perfect Confidence

Jan Ferguson

All you need to get it right first time

- Do you find it hard to stay calm under pressure?
- Are you worried that you don't always stand up for yourself?
- Do you want some straightforward advice on overcoming insecurities?

Perfect Confidence is the ideal companion for anyone who wants to boost their self-esteem. Covering everything from communicating clearly to handling conflict, it explains exactly why confidence matters and equips you with the skills you need to become more assertive. Whether you need to get ahead in the workplace or learn how to balance the demands of friends and family, *Perfect Confidence* has all you need to meet challenges head on.

The *Perfect* series is a range of practical guides that give clear and straightforward advice on everything from getting your first job to choosing your baby's name. Written by experienced authors offering tried-and-tested tips, each book contains all you need to get it right first time.

BOOKS

Perfect Detox

Gill Paul

All you need to feel great every time

- Are you concerned that your eating habits are not as healthy as they should be?
- Do you often feel bloated and sluggish?
- Would you like some expert advice on how to detox safely and effectively?

Perfect Detox is is the ideal companion for anyone who wants to give their system a spring clean. Covering everything from 24-hour cleanses to full 30-day programmes, it gives step-by-step guidance on choosing the right detox plan and helpful advice to ensure that you get the full range of nutrients every day. With a unique A–Z listing that includes nutritional information about over 100 detox superfoods, *Perfect Detox* has everything you need to revive and rejuvenate yourself.

The *Perfect* series is a range of practical guides that give clear and straightforward advice on everything from getting your first job to choosing your baby's name. Written by experienced authors offering tried-and-tested tips, each book contains all you need to get it right first time.

BOOKS

Perfect Relaxation

Elaine van der Zeil

All you need to keep calm under pressure

- Do you want to take control of your hectic lifestyle?
- Do you want to fight back against stress?
- Would you like some tips on how to be more relaxed?

Perfect Relaxation is an invaluable guide for anyone who wants to learn how to remain calm and powerful in challenging situations. Covering everything from how to stop obsessing to how to start thinking positively, it gives step-by-step guidance on beating stress and shows you how to make relaxation a part of your everyday life. With helpful suggestions for instant calming techniques and daily exercises to help combat tension, *Perfect Relaxation* has everything you need to bring your stress levels under control.

BOOKS